I0234346

DeArabizing Arabia

Tracing Western Scholarship on the History of the Arabs and Arabic Language and Script

Saad D. Abulhab

Blautopf Publishing
New York ~ Ulm
blautopfpublishing.com

Blautopf Publishing
New York ~ Ulm
blautopfpublishing.com

Copyright © 2011 by Saad D. Abulhab
All rights reserved, including right of reproduction in whole or in part, in any form.

Colophon
English text set in *Arabic Typesetting* Latin, designed by John Hudson.
Arabic text set in *Jalil, Sabine,* and *Yasmine* fonts, designed by the author.
Headings text set in *Adobe Garamond Premier Pro*, designed by Robert Slimbach.
Greek text set in *SBL Greek*, designed by John Hudson.

Cover Art and Design by the Author
Visualized image featuring the ruined three-story high head statue of the Arab founder of Baghdad, *Abū Ja'far al-Mansūr*, once stood prominently in one of the city's major squares before it was blasted and dumped a few years after the Western-led invasion of Iraq in 2003.

Publisher's Cataloging-in-Publication Data

Abulhab, Saad D.
DeArabizing Arabia : tracing Western scholarship on the history of the Arabs and Arabic language and script / Saad D. Abulhab.
p. cm.
1. Arabic Alphabet–History. 2. Writing, Arabic–History. 3. Arabic Language–History. 4. Inscriptions, Nabataean 5. Inscriptions, Arabic. 6. Arabs–History. 7. Learning and Scholarship–Europe. 8. Koran–History. 9. Muhammad, Prophet, d. 632. I. Title.
PJ6123.A285 2011
492.711–dc22
Library of Congress Control Number: 2011918949
CIP

ISBN: 978-0-9849843-0-5

First Edition

19 17 15 13 12 9 8 7 6 5 4 3 2

DEDICATION

In memory of my father, Dr. Jalil Karim Abulhab, an American-educated Iraqi scientist, author, and scholar, a proud Arab, and an admirer of Western Civilization's contributions and true cultural and humanistic values.

I dedicate this book to the remarkable and indispensible research and contributions by the scholars of the Islamic Arab Civilization era in all fields of human knowledge, including the history of the Arabs and Arabic Language and Script.

CONTENTS

Acknowledgments

Although an author gets the credit for writing a book, others are usually instrumental in its creation. I want to thank them.

I want to thank my book editor, Bassim Jabbar, who did not only help me articulate my thoughts clearly on its pages, but went beyond to reinforce my arguments eloquently, if needed.

I want to thank my brother, O. A. Abulhab for providing me with many clear images of *al-Namārah* inscription during his visit to the Louvre Museum in Paris.

I want to thank Saadi Youssef, the leading Arabic poet, for examining my reading of a key poem line in *Alfiyyat Ibn Mālik*, a poetic summary of the Arabic language grammar.

I want to thank Dennis Carter for giving me the opportunity to trace and read the *Sa'adTa'lib* inscription.

I want to thank my ex-student assistant at Baruch College, Hassan Jamil, for preparing many figures in this book.

I want to thank the Research Foundation of the City University of New York (RF-CUNY) for their generous grants over the years to support my research and publications in the fields of Arabic script history, typography and computing.

I also want to thank the anonymous reviewers of the JNES, JAOS, JSS, AAE, and JAIS publications for rejecting my research papers which prompted me to write this book, and for their valuable comments which helped me confirm my tracings and readings, and further validate my conclusions.

Finally, I am very grateful to my dear wife for 23 years, S. Gruber, the mother of my two beautiful daughters, for copyediting the entire book, patiently, and for her continued support and encouragement.

Preface

Today, any nation whose millennial past, civilizational legacy, geographical prominence, and significant influence on the course of world history are comparable to those of the Arabs, can easily be identified with a specific country or homeland encompassing the majority of its people and named accordingly. Yet, in the case of the Arabs, something is noticeably absent; that is, where is Arabia? Is it Saudi Arabia— named as such after the clan name of its founder King Abd al-Aziz al-*Saud?* Is it Iraq, Syria, Morocco, or Egypt? The Library of Congress listed only two authorized subject headings for Arabia, "Arabia, Southern" and "Arabia, Roman," but not Arabia! Even Saudi Arabia is carefully listed as "Saudi Arabia," not "Arabia, Saudi" or "Arabia (Saudi)," as in the case of "Germany (East)," "Germany (West)," "Russia (Federation)," or "Iran. Islamic Republic." One wonders, when the American journalist and entertainer Lowell Thomas spoke of Arabia, in his famous 1920s book and narrated film about the desert exploits of British Royal Air Force Lieutenant Colonel T. E. Lawrence (widely hailed for his role in organizing the early 19th century Arab Revolt against the Ottomans, earning him international fame as an "Arabian Knight," the "Uncrowned King of Arabia," and "Lawrence of Arabia,") what Arabia did he have in mind? Was he referring to the early twentieth century Arabia as defined by the actual facts of demography, geography, and culture, to a historical Arabia, or to an undefined Arabia that would fit well in a "witty" and "romantic" drama about British colonialism?

Luckily, the uncertainty of Arabia *in the Western Scholarly circles* was clearly explained by Lawrence himself, an esteemed Arabist and an accomplished Near East history and archaeology scholar who graduated with high honors from Oxford. Lawrence wrote in his autobiography that tribesmen and townsmen of Arabic-speaking Asia are of a different race, not "just men in different social and economic stages," because there is no "family resemblance" in the "working of their minds." In other words, when Arab tribes settle in one of the many historically established population centers of the greater Arabian Peninsula, they cease to be Arabs. It follows that Arabia is *indeed* undefined: one is in Arabia when in the vast desert, and outside Arabia when in towns or countryside! Lawrence, an admiring expert of the history of European Crusaders, supported his bizarre classification of the Arabs—which, as will be demonstrated later in this book, conforms well to the core theses of mainstream Western scholarship regarding the

Arabs and Arabia,—by further claiming that his subjects, the Arabs, "were a limited, narrow-minded people, whose inert intellects lay fallow in incurious resignation." "Their imaginations were vivid, but not creative." "They have no organizations of mind or body. They invented no systems of philosophy, no complex mythologies."

If the value of historical research and investigation is to highlight and verify past events and their impact on the life and future of nations, then a research about the history of Arabia should begin by investigating its past based on analytical verifications, not crypto-conclusions generated in-line with an established vision. That is why in the course of this book I tried to emphasize four facts: First, researchers should act to accredit to Arabia its historical significance and civilizational place in history. Second, if the United States, Australia, etc. can claim that their current vital milieus are the product of several hundred years of historical accumulation, then most certainly the Arabs have every right to claim that their current vital milieu is the product of several thousand years of significant historical accumulation. Third, adhering to dialectical analysis, researches should define Arabia, therefore, as the collective homeland of the Arabs regardless of present status of disintegration. Fourth, this implies that Arabia is a geo-physical entity with myriad connected cultures, and myriad groups of peoples and ethnicities united by history and bonded by destiny. This is neither about nationalism nor about romantic infatuation with an abstract idea of justice. Indeed, Arabia —

people and language — has been in existence since the dawn of recorded time, and that despite the facts that some of its boundaries had been changed by invaders at some points in history. This book, therefore, is about this Arabia as historically developed to its current form, boundaries, and states.

Noting that historians, archeologists, and religious scholars can play a major role to advance or justify a given vision, a mutual dialectic relation between that vision and its users comes into existence. Scholarly work in the field of Near East studies is no exception. To the detriment of rigorous archeological studies of the Near East, many of the current Western theories and conclusions regarding the history of the Arabs and their language and script (supposedly based solely on physical evidence) are assumptive and inaccurate. In effect, these theories appear to de-Arabize Arabia and its people and re-invent their history. Scholarly theories in this field do not only exist in textbooks. Throughout the history of the Near East, empires and peoples clashed violently to implement a particular scholarly vision or use it to justify their exploits. Taking advantage of modern-day Western theories regarding the Near East, various ethnical and religious minorities of the Arab world hurried to claim exclusive descendent and ancestry rights to the Nubians, Sumerians, Assyrians, Phoenicians and other legitimate historical groups discussed in these theories, depicting themselves as the "original people" and the Arabs as the "outsiders" of the adjacent Arabian Deserts.

Committed-to-truth researchers should bear in mind that navigating through the many claims and theories regarding Arabia today may require additional efforts to distinguish between what is based on facts and what is driven by a particular established scholarly vision (Western or Islamic Arab.) Incidentally, it is not important that a scholar be of a specific background, or is aware (or unaware) that his beliefs are indeed advocating a particular vision. In the case of western scholarship, what is important is a scholar's adherence to the notion that only modern western theories are scientific enough to be considered reliable, and as such they should be the basis of any research in this field.

When scholars downplay or even exclude important classic Arabic linguistic tools that are necessary for reading ancient inscriptions from Yemen, and when they summarily dismiss centuries of scholarly research from the Islamic Arab civilization era regarding the history of the Arabs and their language, then, we should question whether they are advocating a particular vision — religious, economic, political, etc. Over the years, we observed, more than we could count, that even discussions about the Arabic script and typography could quickly evolve into historical, political, or religious contentions following biased ideological routes where the final intent is the discrediting of the Arab history and its details. What is more baffling, we reached the point in which the mere use of a term such as "Arabic Calligraphy" can draw interminable strings of objections.

The centerpiece of Western scholarship's theme regarding Arabia, and the field of Arabic language and script history seems to be that the classic Arabic language, the modern Arabic script, and even the Arabs themselves, are the youngest of the Near East and were not originated from Yemen as scholars of the Arab Islamic era told us; even more, that people of pre-Islamic Yemen were not Arabs and did not speak Arabic! Contrary to many historical facts, Western theories seem to portray the Arabs as marginal groups of rootless Bedouins and outsiders in their own historical homeland. When I say, historical facts, I do not mean assertions, but historical documents supported by volumes of scholarly work authored by well-accomplished scholars — ancient and modern. It is not surprising, therefore, to see that whenever such facts are mentioned in a research, some Western scholarship circles would react with anger and political accusations and rejection of publication would follow.

Without providing any solid proof, many Western scholars portray the structurally sophisticated and vocabulary-rich classic Arabic language, as a post-Islamic creation. And others go even further: knowing such claims would not stand against the clear evidence of the highly developed language of the Quran (let alone the eloquent pre-Islamic Arabic poetry,) they resort to spreading unsubstantiated theories claiming that both the authenticity of the language of the Quran and its origins are questionable.

It is important to state here that Western scholars are not alone in questioning old Islamic Arab scholarship regarding the history of the Arabs and their language and script. Still, due to their methodical research, organized work, and academic contributions, Western scholars are viewed favorably and habitually considered as a reliable source of information. Thus, their theories could be accepted easily and globally since they are perceived as truthful and academic. This observation is especially accurate, when we consider that these theories are usually presented in peer-reviewed research papers, which often acquire the reputation for being factual reference material.

The subject of Near East studies is complex due to many factors. It is my academic persuasion, therefore, that to fully demonstrate the validity of my observations and conclusions, I have to examine both the evidence presented by the inscriptions and the role played by Western Near East scholarship in the formation of the current belief system in the field, which was mainly shaped by religious and colonial attitude. Scrutinizing modern Western theories about Arabia, the Arabs, and the Arabic language and script is, therefore, an important step to successfully study this correlated and highly disputed topic. I intend this book to be a balanced reference discussing all related topics in this field without observing any artificially imposed guidelines to confine it to the sole discussion of technical matters.

Most of this book is allocated to present my findings and in-depth readings of major relevant inscriptions, which I accumulated in over one and a half year of research. Particularly, I demonstrated in this book that an accurate reading of old Nabataean and Musnad inscriptions would only be possible if we *primarily* utilize the tools of the Classic Arabic language. For example, in my new comprehensive readings of the important *Umm al-Jimāl* and *al-Namārah* Nabataean inscriptions, I concluded based on substantial evidence that *al-Namārah* was not the burial stone of King *Umru'ū al-Qays* or even about him as currently believed, and that *Umm al-Jimāl* was not the burial stone of *Fahrū bin Sālī* but *Faru' bin Sālī.* It is my hope that these new tracings and readings of important historical references, and other findings, would not only inspire more scholarly research and discussions, but also amend several historical and linguistic assumptions.

Initially, I planned to publish this book as "Part One" of a comprehensive textbook on Arabic script history, typography, and computing. However, I decided later to publish each part as a separate monograph to maintain better focus and support specialized readership. As for organizing this book, I divided it in five virtually independent chapters. The first two chapters are intended as introductory essays regarding the history of Arabia (people and language) and the role of Western scholarship. The last three chapters —the core of this book — will present my research findings and conclusions.

Although I conceived major portions of this book to be a reference tool for scholars and researchers, other readers may find the topics and research herewith presented valid enough to debate and to study further. I have to point out though that when reading the technical parts of the book, one needs to be familiar with Nabataean, Musnad, Arabic, Greek, and Aramaic scripts, in addition to early Kufic. All chapters can be read independently. Furthermore, to facilitate the selective and independent reading of the last three chapters, I included (in addition to the chapter-specific selected bibliographies and endnotes already offered throughout the whole book) chapter-specific introductions and conclusions.

CHAPTER 1

Arabia, Islam, and Western Scholarship in Perspective

Although the Arabs built impressive isolated kingdoms and civilizations many centuries before Islam, the advent of this religion remains the most important element that marked the development of their history and national character. It is my conclusion that a scholarly research dealing with the history of the Arabs, Arabia, and the Arabic language and scripts would be, therefore, incomplete without discussing Islam and the way it is perceived by scholars of both the Christian West and the Islamic East. In this chapter, I will provide the reader with a brief and balanced historical account of this important topic. In addition, I will undertake a frank discussion about the controversial and speculative Western theories, old and new, regarding the Quran and Muhammad. It is important to emphasize that serious researchers should never prejudge scholarship and theories, Western or Islamic, in this particular field as being impartial. One needs to evaluate, therefore, any such theories, particularly modern-day mainstream Western theories, within their defining environment: history.

Aside from being a religion, Islam was the inspirational motive that led to the first successful unification of the Arabian Peninsula into an organized political state. Under Islam, the Arabs defeated the two major military powers that for centuries competed for dominance over their lands: the Romans and the Persians. After Islam became the prevailing religion, Arabia emerged as an independent regional power and a principle player in empire building and civilization. Aside from transforming the lives of the Arabs, the progressive teachings of Islam, taken in a historical perspective, greatly influenced neighboring nations. Contrary to the believes of many scholars in the West, the massive conversion of the Arabs and non-Arabs to Islam was not significantly due to military expansionism, but mainly to the power of a new culture, advanced moral principles, and to appropriate solutions to social problems.

The powerful message of Islam, from inception to present time, remains appealing to millions of people living as far as Indonesia, the largest Muslim nation today. It is a fact that in the case of Indonesia, Islam became the dominant religion without a sword — a term preferred by some Western scholars to describe Islamic expansions.

To focus the subject, Islam has never been a nationalist Arab movement or ideology. Defining Islam neutrally and outside the concept of religion is easy: it is a concise collection of universal humanistic philosophies and teachings. Politically, it was its message that successfully united the Arabs and elevated their stance in the region. The idea of an idealistic, humanistic, and multi-ethnic Islamic *Ummah* (nation) that could replace tribal and ethnic-based imperial kingdoms did not pass, however, the test of historical longevity. Arabs, Persians, Turks, and others who climbed the ladder of Islamic power after the death of the last elected Muslim leader, *'Ali bin Abī Ṭālib*, had each done their share of ethnic chauvinism and paternalism to weaken the nascent Islamic state thus leading to its eventual demise. Today, the notion of a unified Islamic state is outdated. In fact, countries with Islamic majorities are politically independent and ethnically dominated nation-states. Nonetheless, the concept of Islamic *Ummah* (Islamic nation) continues to be a powerful call for unity, solidarity, cooperation, and peaceful coexistence. Above all, that concept has become a driving force for national resistance against foreign domination that continues unabated until modern days. It is not farfetched to say that, the appealing Islamic call for unity and resistance against tyranny and injustice is probably the main factor behind the enmity of those targeting Islam and Muslims in Arabia and elsewhere.

1.1 Religion, Colonial History, and Western Scholarship

Religion and European colonial history are independent fields of study. As such, they may not necessarily belong to a research book on the history of the Arabs and Arabic language and script. However, investigating a scholarly work (Western or Islamic Arab) within its defining socio-historical environment does belong, due to its multiple cultural and theoretical implications and consequences. Examining theories and conclusions of a scholarly work outside their generating matrixes would make no sense. Furthermore, claiming that an established vision could be driving some of the academic research on the languages of the Near East with Arabic at the center should not be construed as a call for academic conflict as such a prospect might lead to futile criticism and fruitless discussion. However, professional commitment to academic research warrants that we address this complex subject in its totality by incorporating useful or relevant facts of history.

Discussing the impact of religious and sociological factors in the West — at the time when many modern theories about the history of Arabia and its languages were established — is important in one respect. Since among the objectives of this book is to point out that modern-day Western theories about the Arabic language and scripts run contrary to the indisputable evidence that emerged from studying inscriptions, such discussion would be essential in that it would enable us to question the vision behind these theories and to dispute their accuracy.

Western Christian scholarship, like Islamic Arab scholarship, played a decisive role in shaping world history. Neither scholarship is limited to dealing with purely theoretical topics that are removed from everyday governing decisions. Throughout history, and particularly after the Roman Empire adapted Christianity, religion-inspired scholarship was at the center stage in many world events. Following the path sketched by religious scholars and their theories, millions of troops marched under the flags of religions and fought to their rhythms and tunes. Not surprisingly, while scholars helped shaping historical events, the events themselves helped shaping their work.

With regard to the history of the Arabian Peninsula and particularly the history of the Fertile Crescent, theories and assumptions by the European Christians clashed directly with those of the Islamic Arab civilization era. This is expected since prior to the unification of Arabia after the rise of Islam, the Europeans had many centuries of dominant imperial presence in the region, which started with the arrival of the Greek colonists in Asia Minor. [9] For a variety of reasons, including religion and history, the Europeans had never accepted the realities of Arabia — people and geography — particularly after Islam. On the other hand, and as we will discuss later, the Arabs before and after Islam have always seen the Arabian Peninsula, including the Fertile Crescent, as their undisputed homeland. Their longing to see their homeland united was one of the main factors behind their embracing of Islam. Earlier, the Arabs have rallied for many centuries to protect their existence in the vast, harsh, and very difficult-to-protect open lands of the Arabian Peninsula.

Without a doubt, during the dark ages, the European Christian vision and scholarship were the driving force behind the Crusaders' military campaign in the Near East. Indeed, the European Crusaders have added a new ideological dimension to the older Roman exercise of empire building and to the practice of colonial conquest in general, namely religion. Initially, they eyed just Palestine, the birthplace of Jesus. Later though, and over two hundred years of warfare to expand their colonies beyond Palestine, their goal became evident: *to control most of the western Fertile Crescent (currently greater Syria and Iraq) and to de-Arabize and de-Islamize the Near East.* Despite their failure to hold on Jerusalem, the Crusaders campaign succeeded eventually in accomplishing a more significant victory: ending the Abbasid Caliphate of Baghdad, which played a key role in maintaining unity and protecting the Muslim Arab civilization, globally.

A brief review of key history facts, which are not even mentioned in most history textbooks today, is essential to illustrate my preceding observation. In all their sweeping attacks across the Asian plains, mountains, and deserts, the Mongols from Genghis Khan to Tamerlane were never driven by ideology or interested in imposing their cultural values. Ironically, most ended up converting to Islam and Christianity, mingled with the conquered people thus forming new ethnic groups, and adapted the local languages wherever they settled.

However, and only as an exception, after the Mongols sacked Baghdad, in February 1258, and after an immense carnage lasting over six months that claimed over two million victims, they added one more dimension to their onslaught. They burned down symbols of culture: schools and libraries; destroyed symbols of the Islamic religion: mosques; and killed or enslaved most scholars and scientists they managed to put hands on.

Unlike all other typical Mongol attacks elsewhere, the sacking of Baghdad was deliberately planned and carried out by a joint Christian Mongol force, with the familiar ideological theme of the European crusaders. Hulago was not just another Mongol destroyer; but a Christian Mongol destroyer — unlike his grandfather, Genghis Khan who had kept equal distances from both Christians and Muslims, and had repeatedly rejected earlier Crusaders' requests to coordinate their attacks in the Muslim world. "Hulago was a fanatic adversary of the Muslims." [6] He had a close relationship with his mother, Sorkhokhtani, an influential fervent Nestorian Christian, and even closer relationship with one of his two Christians wives, Dakuz (or Tokuz) Khatun, who was described by Syriac Christian sources as "the believing Queen, and a true Christian, who raised up the horn of the Christians in all the earth." As a matter of fact, Mongol women had administered the vast

Mongol empire while men went off to their years-long war campaigns. Following the short reign of her husband (1227-1229 CE,) Hulago's mother, the widow of Genghis Khan's youngest son, Tolui, became the actual ruler of China and Eastern Mongolia, for more than twenty years. [14]

Tokus was Hulago's father's wife, but he took her to wife according to the customs of the Mongols. "She died during the days of summer, in the year her husband died, and there was great mourning among the Christians throughout the world at the departure of these two great lights, who made the Christian Faith to triumph. Hulago had for a long time wished to marry Mary, a daughter of Michael VIII Palaeologos (1261-83), and the princess was dispatched to Mongolia in due course. According to some authorities, Hulago died soon after her arrival, and according to others she did not arrive until after his death, when she became the wife of Abhaka, Hulagu's son and successor." [14]

In fact, many of Hulago's fighters and important military leaders were Christians from the Caucasus European region. "Among those offering an alliance to Hulago was Hayton, the Christian king of Armenia. Hayton regarded the Mongols' invasion as a new crusade to free Jerusalem from the Muslims, who had retaken the city from the Crusaders only recently, in 1244. His perception was encouraged by Hulago's chief lieutenant, Kitbuqa, who was not only a Christian, but also claimed to be a direct descendant of one of the three Magi who had brought gifts to the infant Jesus. Following his visit to the Mongol leader, Hayton sent messages to his Crusader neighbors that Hulago was about to be baptized a Christian, and strongly urged that they too ally themselves with this new force, and turn it to the Crusader cause." When Hulago entered the surrendering city of Damascus, he was accompanied by Kitbuqa, Hayton, and Bohemond IV, the Crusader prince of Antioch. [12]

Earlier, ahead of his advance toward Baghdad, Hulago "forged secret ties to the Christians within the city" and throughout the Middle East. After Hulago's army defeated the Muslim Arab troops defending the besieged city, he "sent his Christian troops into the city to collect the boot." By his order, "the churches and Christian property in the city remained secure from plunder and Hulago presented one of the Caliph's palaces to the Catholikos Makikha," the patriarch of the Christian church in Iraq; "the Christians were spared, and shut up in one of the quarters of the city, whilst he laid waste all the other quarters." Local Christians inside Baghdad "joined their fellow believers to loot the city and slaughter the Muslims." The looting lasted seventeen to forty days during which the invaders set the city afire, while they "defiled and destroyed mosques, and turned many of them into churches." They were allowed by Hulago "to destroy the tombs of the long line of Abbasid Caliphs." In an unparalleled exception to the Mongol tradition throughout their vast captured territories, "Hulago exempted the Christian priests from kowtowing at the court since they bowed only to God." [6][14]

With the fall of Baghdad and up to present time, the Arabs had lost the ability to lead their own destiny and to play any significant role in shaping events in their own homeland — in fact they reverted to their pre-Islamic "dark age" state of affairs. Less than a century later, the rich Islamic Arab scholarly contributions, to all fields of human knowledge, trickled down, before they practically disappeared. Arabia went back to its status as a divided land of city-states, fiefdoms, and kingdoms desperate for protection from powerful players in the region: the Turks, Persians, and eventually the Europeans. The Fertile Crescent became, as it was before Islam, a contested land and a battleground between those in the East (the Persians) and those in the north (the Romans.) (Interestingly, the Iraqis, and Arabs in general, have historically and traditionally referred to the Ottoman Turks as "the Romans," too, because they came from the north.) [13]

The extent to which past European and Islamic Arab scholars differed on the nature and teachings of Islam, as well as on the history and territorial integrity of Arabia can never be told as clearly and loudly as the above mentioned violent history reveals. It would be assumptive and even naïve to study the 19th century European theories about the history of Arabia and the Arabs separately from the historical environment of only several centuries earlier — especially since this violent history was mainly shaped by the European Christian scholarly vision, the dominant vision of the 19th century Europe and even of the modern-day West. In fact, one cannot help but to observe with astonishment the repeating carnages and catastrophic devastation unfolding in Iraq before and after the Western-led invasion in 2003, which, *despite all other factors*, was greatly inspired by this same religious scholarly vision. A quick reading of the post-occupation Iraqi constitution clearly reveals that deArabizing Iraq is a prime goal.

To be accurate, the 19th century European colonialists had more important reasons than the Crusaders to pursue their goals of domination. With that being said, religion and particularly the Christian scholarship vision were still high on that list of reasons. Technically and as an ideology, they never abandoned it. Before the so-called European enlightenment era, Western Scholarship regarding the Near East was substantially linked to religion. After the rise of modern colonialism, this association became less apparent, transforming into a more settled, complex, and realistic one.

On the arrival of the 19th century European colonialism in Arabia, it seemed that the Europeans had put the violent history of the region behind them. Their scholarly vision was not solely based on religious teachings anymore. In fact, the great work of Western historians and archeologists of that period had revealed for the first time much of what we know today about the ancient history of the region. Even more, they have worked hard to revive much of the lost scholarly work of the past Islamic Arab civilization era. Even local Islamic scholars of the Middle East embraced their work. Still, a researcher in this field should not confuse the accuracy and importance of modern-age discoveries accomplished by the western scholars with a presumed accuracy of their assumptions, hypothesis, and conclusions — regularly presented as factual and based solely on the merit of these discoveries. Despite their great technical contributions in the fields of Near East archeology and history, one should observe that most of the theoretical conclusions made by these accomplished Western scholars are supporting, or at least non-conflicting with, their religious believes.[5][11]

1.2 Muhammad and the Quran: A Brief Balanced Account

A serious and honest discussion of modern-day Western theories regarding the history of Arabia and the Arabic language and script cannot be achieved without impartially examining the two most important defining factors and references in the history of the Arabs and their language: Muhammad's leadership and the Quran.

It is intellectually and scholarly understandable that people could challenge the teachings of Muhammad or the Quran because of conflict in cultural values or inherited traditions. However, questioning the authenticity of the Quran and Muhammad, and the integrity of the Arabic language, used to express Muhammad's teaching and the contents of the Quran, should necessarily be cross-examined in any pertinent textbook. Arriving to conclusions drastically differing from those presented within volumes of research by the scholars of the Islamic Arab civilization era does not only contradict with the nature of scholarly research as a continual process, but has the potential to re-write history to suit a purpose.

Aside from rigid monotheism that shares with Judaism and Christianity, the belief in creationism and the supremacy of one God, two inseparable pillars support the Islamic faith: Muhammad and the Quran. This explains the reasons behind the over a thousand-year-old tenacity with which some extremist elements in the West continued to attack Muhammad and his legacy. Beginning from the dawn of Islam and peaking with Pope Urban II, who called for the liberation of *Hierosolyma* (Jerusalem-al-Quds) from the "Muslim infidels," the attacks against Muhammad and the Quran never stopped until this very day. They called him the "Antichrist;" they called him "impostor" and "founder of a heresy," and they said he "wearied the Patience and Long-Suffering of God." In the Middle Ages, Europeans of Jewish faith called him "*ha-meshuggah,*" *meaning* "possessed" as used in the Hebrew Bible. Martin Luther, the founder of Lutheranism, called him, "a devil and first-born child of Satan."[15] After 9/11, a very influential American Christian Evangelist preacher, Jerry Falwell, called Muhammad "terrorist", Ayaan Hirisi Ali called him a "pervert and terrorist", and another American Christian Evangelist preacher, Pat Robertson, called him "sex deviant and a pervert". [7] Even before Nine-eleven, a mediocre Indian author, Salman Rushdie, gained international notoriety and Western admiration for calling Muhammad's revelations in the Quran, "Satanic Verses."

Born in Mecca on April 26th 570 CE to a leading clan, *Muḥammad bin 'Abd Allāh bin 'Abd al-Muṭṭalib*, is a real person whose existence is documented beyond any doubt. His birth involved no miracles and he claimed no magical skills. Quoting his words, he was an earthly human like all other men. We know as much, if not tremendously more, detailed information about his personal life than we know about all Roman, Persian, Greek, and other historical thinkers and leaders of the old world.

Muhammad was not just another prophet whose existence is presumed when reading sacred books as in the case of prophets often cited in the Ibrahimian (Abrahamic) faiths. Incontrovertible evidence, including manuscripts and inscriptions, attests to Muhammad's existence, words, teachings, and deeds. We can even locate the homes he lived in, the paths he traveled, and where he was buried. From scholarly, independent position, the study of the life and leadership of Muhammad would attest that he possessed unsurpassed talent and vision that should qualify him to be one of a handful top leaders and thinkers ever known.

Observing human suffering, Muhammad chose involvement rather than the easy spiritual isolation typically adopted by religious leaders of his time. He preached public interest rather than tribal interest. He believed in people just as he believed in God. He did not shy away from taking responsibility and painful decisions. As a political leader, he had no illusions about his enemies and friends. To his credit, he excelled as a leader of a secretive movement for more than a decade in a very hostile environment.

After migration (*Hijra*) to *Yathrib* (Medina) to escape persecution, he demonstrated superior governing skills, and laid the foundation for a new powerful state formed around revolutionary and enlightened egalitarian concepts. Above all, he was a genius military commander who personally directed the battles to unify Arabia. He won 26 battles out of 28, some of them against far more experienced armies, like the Byzantine army. [3] Instead of establishing a monarchic state, Muhammad preached and established a relatively democratic state. He made sure not to name any one to lead after him, and asked his followers to elect a new leader by consultation. As a leader in charge of the immense wealth of Medina, he lived modestly and did not indulge himself as most kings and leaders of his time. Muhammad was the archetype of an anti-tribal man living in an inflexibly tribal society. He disliked ethnic chauvinism. Unlike other ethnically dominated kingdoms and empires of his time, Muhammad was the first leader to envision and practice a multiethnic state where people are treated equally, regardless of their origin and race. He explicitly preached that there was no difference among people except that of their deeds.

Married to just one wife until her death, he enforced the marriage limit of four wives, coupled with very difficult conditions to fulfill, in a society where women were treated as objects and men were able to marry unlimited number of women. All of Muhammad's marriages after the death of his first wife, *Khadījah bint Khūwaylid*, were for pure political purposes to build alliances and facilitate conversion to Islam.

Conclusively, Muhammad should be considered as an important champion of women rights long before such concept came to existence. Under his leadership, the killing of newly born girls (an Asian practice still performed today in some South Asian countries) was outlawed and ended. He gave women a half of the inheritance given to men in a society that did not allow before any inheritance to women. He enabled ordinary women to own land more than a thousand years before the United Kingdom allowed them to do so.

Muhammad was the first state leader ever to preach openly against slavery. He succeeded into making a significant blow to the stubbornly slave-based system when he set an example by freeing his own slaves. He preached against slavery many centuries before Abraham Lincoln did, and at a time when other religions and beliefs did not even want to consider such subject. He even helped one of his former slaves, who became his adopted son upon freedom, to marry one of his cousin's daughters, and allowed another to assume a leadership role. As for the essence of his message, Muhammad was the ultimate moderate who addressed the problems of his society using moderate solutions. In a society where Jews and Christians fought endlessly to claim the sole righteous path, he preached Islam (peace) and recognized both Christianity and Judaism as preceding divine religions. Following a moderate path, he neither avoided responsibility nor sacrificed principles. Muhammad was an ethical and focused man who would not compromise his beliefs and goals. He refused to abandon his message despite tremendous suffering and the attractive offers he received to recant.

Putting religious and ideological debates aside, and speaking purely from a modern scholarly viewpoint, if Muhammad was the miracle leader of Arabia, the Quran, a book as real and as solid as Muhammad himself, was therefore the miracle of his Islamic message.

The Quran is not just another "holy" book. In fact, the Muslims never refer to the Quran as *al-Qurān al-Muqaddas* (the Holy Quran), but as *al-Qurān al-Karīm* (the Generous Quran.) Among its other scholarly values, the Quran should be looked at as one of the earliest codified constitutions ever written. Muhammad paid extra efforts to make sure that the words of the Quran were recorded precisely as he delivered them to avoid both alteration and adulteration. The Quran, which was recorded in a relatively brief period, was conceived to remain unaltered to differentiate it from other religious books recorded over many centuries and that were written by several authors such as the Torah and the Bible.

The Quran is a book with topics that deal with life and afterlife. It emphasizes that it was delivered in a clear and concise language to make it understandable to the people of Arabia. The Surah of *al-Nisā'*, for example, details with astounding precision how inheritance works under an Islamic state. Indeed, the introduction of the Quran in Arabia marked the beginning of scholarship on many fronts. Following the example provided therein, Muslim, non-Muslim, Arab, and non-Arab scholars made impressive advances in all fields of science and knowledge.

Considering its unique eloquence, the Quran should be treated as the epitome of scholarly treasures, and as a crucial reference and evidence of the history of Arabia and the Arabic language. If an independent scholar were to read the Quran in its formal Arabic language, the first natural conclusion should be this: the language of the Quran is so advanced that its roots must go so deep into the ancient language that was spoken by the majority of the people of the Peninsula at the time of Muhammad. My point: the ultra-sophisticated language of the Quran could not have been invented at the time of Muhammad, or during the Abbasid Caliphate era, or even two millennia before that. Further, it is false that the language of the Quran was merely the language of the people of Mecca. Verb, sentence structure, and construction in the Quran reveal much deeper grammar rules and etymological roots of a language that must have been common to all Arabia. To conclude, a language so articulate and so vocabulary-rich such as that of the Quran could not have been but a result of ages of constant linguistic evolution. In addition, the scholarly evidence that the Quran was not altered beyond insignificant or minor inaccuracies introduced by scribes is overwhelming.

That today's Quran is identical to the one introduced during Muhammad's life is not a religious view but a scholarly academic fact. In examining the wealth of information and the many available copies of older Qurans — with and without diacritic marks and vocalizations — from the first half century after *Hijra*, one concludes that the Quran today is substantially identical to the Quran during Muhammad's life.

The fact that the Arabic Jazm script and writing system were still evolving before, during, and after Muhammad (as we will discuss in chapter 5) can certainly cause minor scriptural errors or differences in various copies of the Quran— scribes can make mistakes. Two script styles, *Mā'il* and the Early Kufic seem to be among the earliest styles that were specifically invented by the Muslim Arabs of Mecca and Medina to record the Quran. It is quite evident that the second style was eventually adopted as the official Quranic script style even before the time of the third Muslim Caliph *'Uthmān bin 'Affān* (579 - 656 CE) who ruled a couple of decades after the passing of Muhammad. All other subsequent copies of the Quran, including those produced in the Abbasid era in Baghdad, which utilized highly transformed Arabic script with elaborate system of diacritic and vocalization marks, were clearly following the earliest edition of the Quran that was organized and recorded in its current form during the reign of Caliph *Uthmān bin 'Affān.*

By randomly comparing many pages from various old Qurans (conserved in various museums and institutes around the world,) with today's Quran, I have positively concluded that these old Quran editions are substantially identical to the Quran edition followed today by all Muslims. The old Quranic samples I compared included pages from the so-called Sanaa Codex and the Berssestrager archive — heavily cited today by some Western scholars as a possible evidence that the Quran was not recorded in a specific period, but evolved into its current form centuries later. A remark is in order. Upon comparing text from about 20 pages from the Sanaa Codex and the Berssestrager archive, including more than 1500 words, with the same text in 5 different copies of present day Qurans, I found only two words with questionable differences: one is related to vocalization, and the other to the total number of verses (*āyah*) in a chapter (*sūrah*). This can be explained since thousands of Arab and non-Arab scribes had re-produced copies of the Quran from Spain to China.

In my comparisons, I used five different Quran editions: Pikthall, *Makhlūf,* King Fahad Quran publications, *Tafsīr al-Jalālayn,* and an old edition edited in its original calligraphy by *al-Shanqītī.* While *al-Shanqītī* and the Berssestrager archive stated that *Sūrat al-Anfāl* has 76 verses, all other editions stated that it has 75 verses. In *Sūrat Ṭāhā*

(20:71), the word ءآمنتم or أأمنتم was identical in *al-Jalālayn, al-Shanqīṭī* and the Berssestrager archive but was written آمنتم in all other editions. Finally, In *Sūrat al-Kahaf* (18:55), the word قِبلاً was identical in *al-Shanqīṭī* and Sana Codex but was written قُبُلاً in all other editions. If anything, my readings of the sample pages of the Sanaa Codex and the Berssestrager archive convinced me that the Quran today is identical to the old ones. To assist the readers, I prepared the table of Figure 1.1 to illustrate the old soft vowel diacritic dotification system (*Ḥarakāt*) that was used with Early Kufic calligraphy style to record the earliest copies of the Quran.

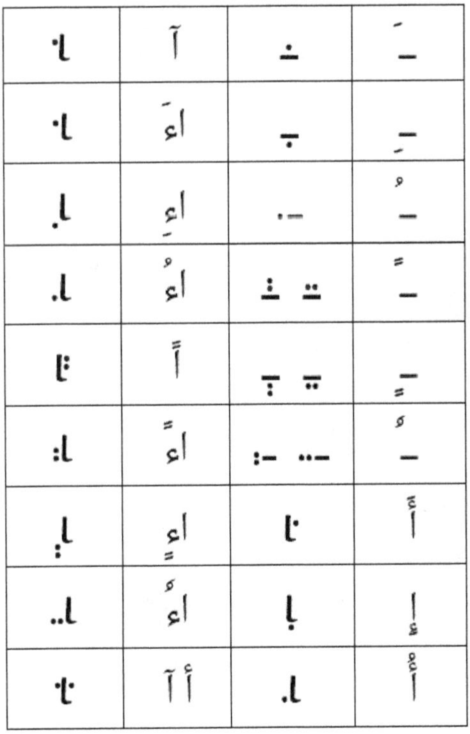

Figure (1.1) A Table illustrating the soft vowel diacritics system (*Ḥarakāt*) used in the Early Kufic Calligraphy style that was utilized in the recording of the earliest copies of the Quran.

Figures 1.2-7 show the sample pages from the Qurans of the Berssestrager archive and the Sanaa Codex, which I selected randomly among many other pages to read, as well as for readers to conduct their own verification.

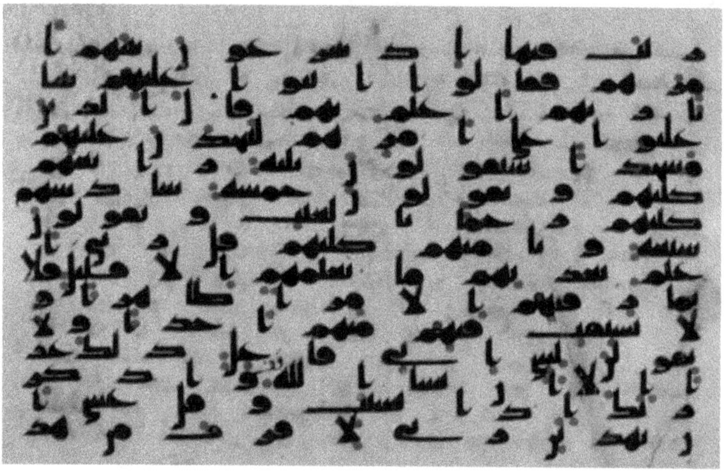

Figure (1.2) *Sūrat al-Kahaf*, Quran (18:21). From Sanaa Codex

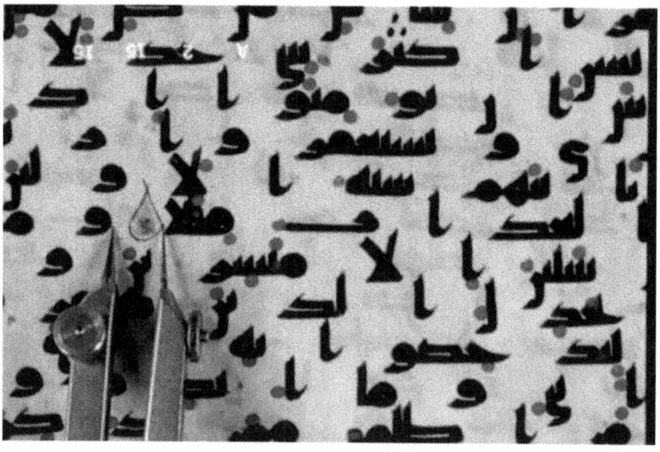

Figure (1.3) *Sūrat al-Kahaf*, Quran (18:54). From Sanaa Codex

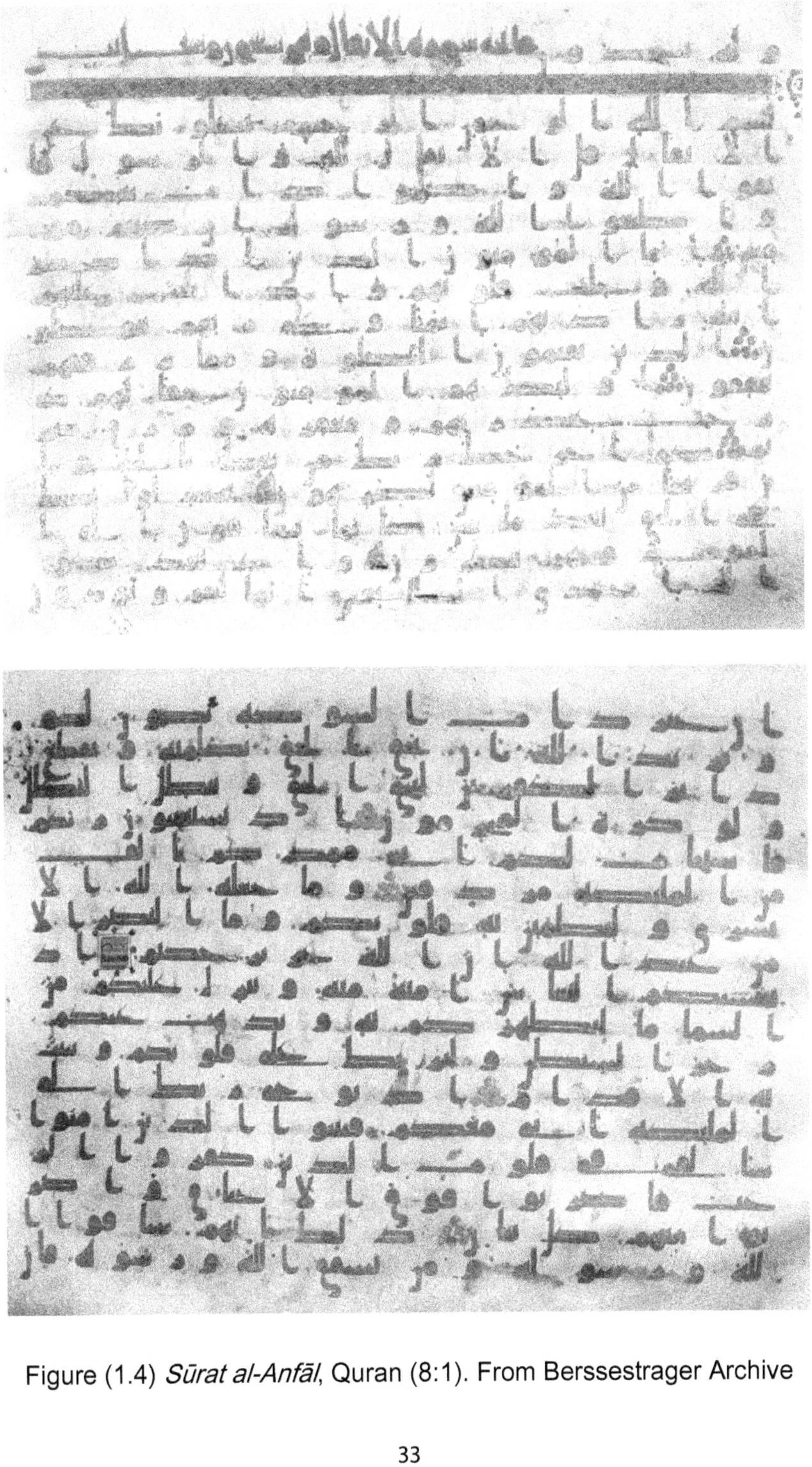

Figure (1.4) *Sūrat al-Anfāl*, Quran (8:1). From Berssestrager Archive

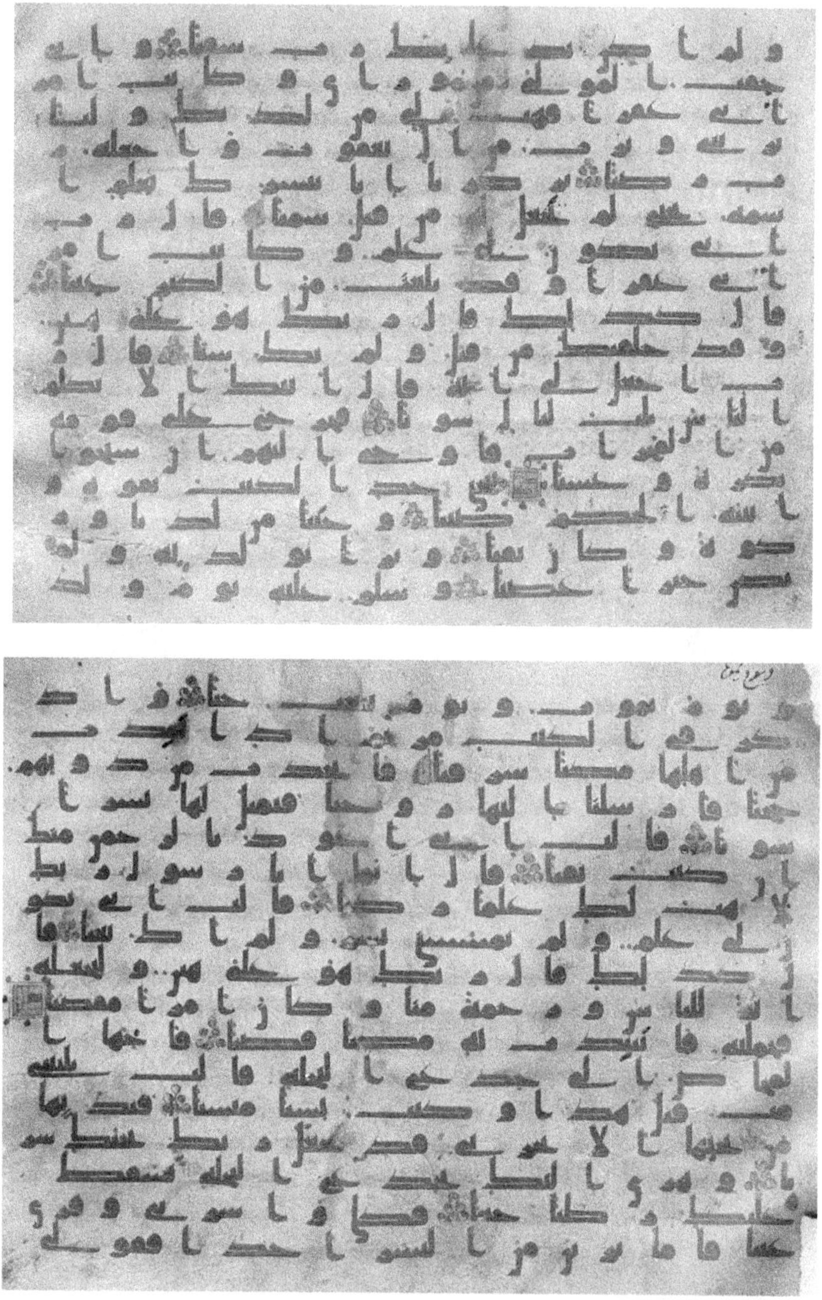

Figure (1.5) *Sūrat Maryam*, Quran (19:4). From Berssestrager Archive

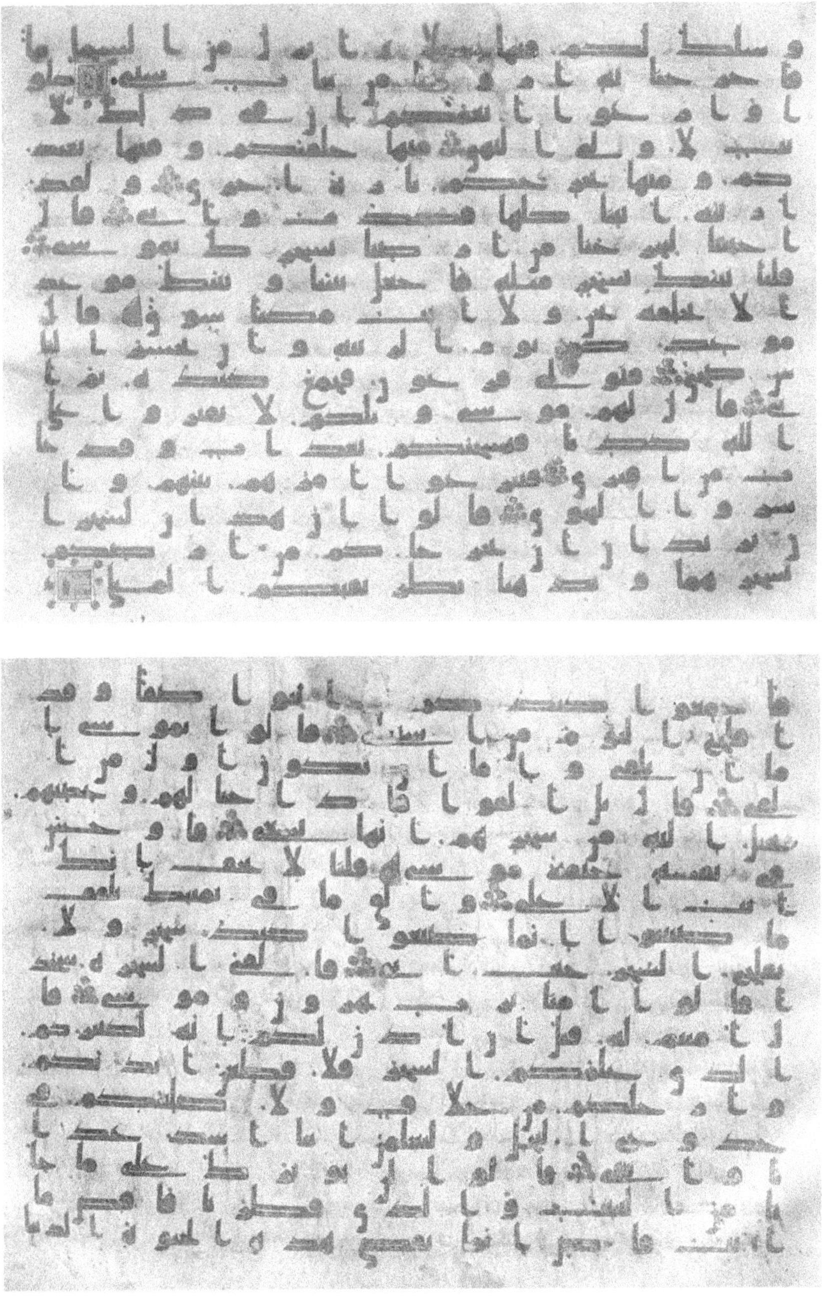

Figure (1.6) *Sūrat Ṭāhā*, Quran (20:58). From Berssestrager Archive

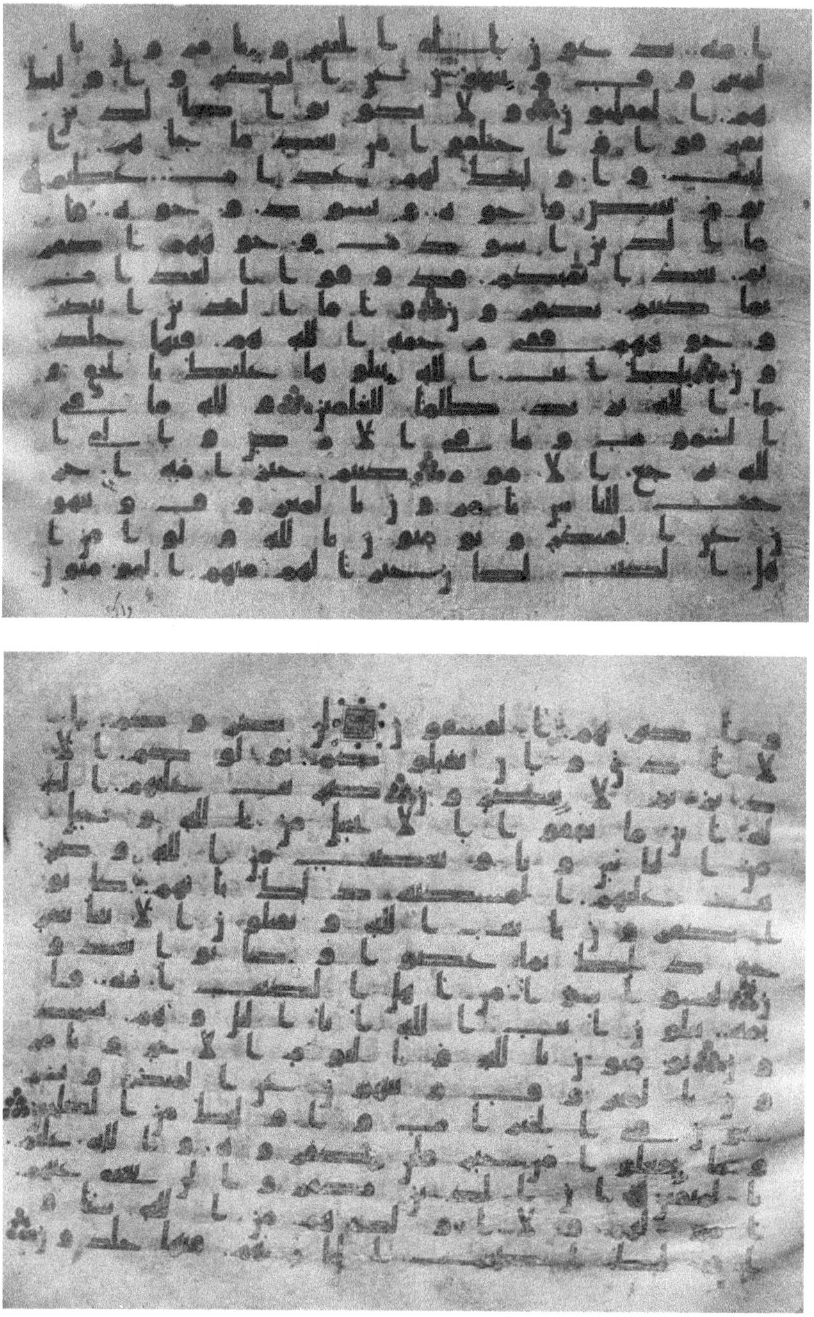

Figure (1.7) *Sūrat Āl 'Umrān*, Quran (3:106) From Berssestrager Archive

Together, the Quran and Muhammad leadership and personality are undeniably the most important historical evidence attesting to Arabia's past, and a key inspirational force for its present and future. However, students and scholars of the Quran and Islamic and Arabic studies should take into account that this field of knowledge is hard to isolate from biased or one-sided scholarly theses. As such, one should fully examine all theses to ascertain competence and verify sources of information. At this point, it would be instructive to present for analysis some of the recently circulated claims put forth by a new but more aggressive generation of Western scholars regarding Muhammad and the Quran.

1.3 The New Trend of Mass Media Scholarship

Before examining the work and theories of this contemporary trend of Western scholarship on the history of Arabia and Arabic language and script, it is worth noting that what distinguishes this trend from past ones is that many powerful semi-scholarly media publications and organizations are actively promoting it. Unfortunately, this trend does not only assault Muhammad and the Quran and, unfairly, discredit the work of countless scholars of the Islamic Arab era, but it also discredit the hard work of many other unbiased and accomplished Western scholars in the field.

Even before the tragedy of Nine-eleven and the subsequent assault on Islam for reasons that go beyond the nature of the event, several amusing theories denying the existence of Muhammad began to circulate. Today, many articles and books questioning the existence of Muhammad or questioning the integrity of the Arabic language of the Quran are introduced on the pages of prominent scholarly journals, magazines and even daily newspapers as a breakthrough scholarly work, sometimes with added humor to gain emotional approval as a means to convince the readers.

As of lately, several elegant books presented Sassanid-Arab coins from the first *Hijrī* decades as a proof that Muhammad was not a real personality but rather a pre-Islamic Persian mythical personality. [8] This sort of deceptive and provocative scholarship can only convince two types of audiences: those with no prior or adequate knowledge of the facts of Islamic history, and those who already have a personal desire to believe them.

For instance, it is a fact that the earliest fully Islamic Arabic coins were produced during the times of the Caliph *Marwān bin 'Abd al-Malik* around 70 *Hijrī*. The production of these coins came after protracted reluctance and deliberation. Reason being, Muslims feared that the abrupt abandonment of Sassanid and Roman coins (which were used as-is or with slight modification in the early decades of Islam) could produce devastating effects on their young economy. The fact that early Muslims used Sassanid coins carrying the word Muhammad is neither new nor unique —there were even Roman Byzantine coins having the engraved name of Muhammad!

The word Muhammad was apparently added by the Muslims utilizing already available Sassanid and Byzantine coin casting equipment for economical and technical reasons. To illustrate this point, we invite the reader to examine the coin images in the two pages of Figure 1.8. These are printouts from a coin collector's catalogue showing early post-Islamic Sassanid and Byzantine coins, which were re-produced with added Islamic Arabic words like *Muḥammad* or *Muḥammad Rasūl Allāh*!

In another example of this noisy, mass media scholarship, We read on November 15, 2008, in an article by Andrew Higgins of the Wall Street Journal titled, *Professor Hired for Outreach to Muslims Delivers a Jolt*, along with a generous excerpt section which was titled, *Excerpt: Muslim Academic Questions Muhammad's Existence*, and was started with the following paragraph:

> *Below are translated excerpts from an article in German entitled, "Islamic Theology without the Historic Muhammad -- Comments on the Challenges of the Historical-Critical Method for Islamic Thinking," by Germany's Prof. Muhammad Kalisch, a Muslim.* [2]

One does not need to comment on Mr. Higgins emphasis that Prof. Muhammad Kalisch, a German Muslim convert, was an academic, a professor, a Muslim, and a German. It is understood why Higgins pointed out these qualities: they can be very helpful in convincing a reluctant reader. Incidentally, Germany, generally known for quality work in most fields,

Sasanian

1 **Shapur I (240-270 AD),** Drachm, no mint, undated, first type for reign, 4.32g. *Good very fine.* £200-250

2 **Varhan I (271-274 AD),** Drachm, no mint, undated, first type for reign, 4.21g. *Good very fine.* £300-350

3 **Artashir III (379-383 AD),** Drachm, GN (Gundishapur) regnal year 2, 2.93g. *Clipped to dirham weight, good very fine.* £200-250

Arab-Sasanian

4 **Khusraw II type,** Drachm, SK (Sistan) year 38?, 3.69g (Walker p.16, ETN.5). *Good very fine.* £200-250

5 **'Abd Allah b. 'Amir (c.41-45h),** Drachm, DR (Darabjird) 43 = 44-47h, 4.07g (Walker p.48:70). *Good very fine.* £200-250

6 **Ziyad b. Abi Sufyan (c.45-55h),** Drachm, NH (Nihawand) 52h, 2.77g (Walker p.42:62). *Clipped to dirham weight, about very fine.* £150-200

7 **Samura b. Jundab (c.52-53h),** Drachm, DA (Darabjird) 43h (frozen date), 3.91g (Walker -; SICA I:244). *Good very fine, rare.* £250-300

8 **'Ubayd Allah b. Ziyad (55-64h),** Drachm, AYRAN (Hulwan?) 30pye, 2.91g (Walker I.23; SICA I:44). *Very fine and very rare.* £150-180

9 **'Abd Allah b. al-Zubayr (60-73h),** Drachm, DA (Darabjird) 59, 3.91g. (Walker -). *Very fine.* £150-200

Figure (1.8) Two pages from a coin collectors' catalogue showing Arabic Sassanid and Byzantine Coins.

10 **'Umar b. 'Ubayd Allah (67-70h),** Drachms (2), ART (Ardashir Khurra), 70h, KRMAN (Kirman) 65h (A 21). *Good very fine and very fine.* (2) £250-350

11 **'Umar b. 'Ubayd Allah,** Drachm, ART (Ardashir Khurra) 70h, 3.66g (Walker p.99:B.34). *Very fine.* £200-250

12 **'Abd Allah b. Umayya (c.74-77h),** Drachm, SK (Sijistan) 75h, 3.99g (SICA -; Gaube 22; A 30). *Very fine, rare.* £250-300

13 **'Abd Allah b. Umayya,** Drachm, SK (Sijistan) 77h, *al-'izza lillah* in obverse margin, 4.04g (Walker -; SICA -). *Very fine and very rare.* £250-300

14 **al-Muhallab b. Abi Sufra (c.75-79h),** Drachm, BISH (Bishapur) 75h, 4.00g (Walker p.114:221). *Good very fine.* £150-200

15 **al-Hajjaj b. Yusuf (75-95h),** Drachm, BISH (Bishapur) 80h, 3.86g (Walker p.120:240, but date 80 not 83). *Good very fine.* £250-300

16 **'Abd al-Rahman b. Muhammad (c.81-84h),** Drachm, SK (Sistan), date unclear (struck c.80-83h), 4.01g (Walker -). *Crude very fine and very rare.* £250-300

17 **Muhammad,** Drachm, mint unidentified (probably in Adharbayjan), date unclear (40ye?), *waf* in *obv* margin, 3.05g (Walker B.39; SICA 494). *Very fine and extremely rare.* £400-600

ARAB-BYZANTINE

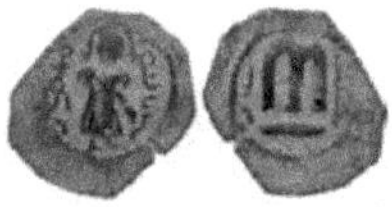

18 Fals, Iliya Filistin, standing caliph, *muhammad rasul allah* to left and right, *rev* **m** with line below, *iliya?* downwards to left and *filastin?* upwards to right, 3.83g (Walker -; SICA -). *Very fine and very rare, apparently an unrecorded variety.* £100-150

seems to be the first choice for most of these new "daring" scholarly theories.

The article described Kalisch as an Islamic theologian, who was a professor of Islamic theology in the Münster University. Prof. Kalisch is entitled, of course, to conduct his research as freely as he wants. However, we do not need to go as far as Tilman Nagel, a Göttingen University scholar and author of a new book, *Muhammad: Life and Legend*, and sign a petition in his support. Nagel justified his action as follows, "We are in Europe," where "Education is about thinking, not just learning by heart." His assumptive elitist statement is self-explanatory and reflects clearly a general Western scholarly attitude toward the work of Muslim scholars — old and new.

By all accounts, some of the recent scholarly questioning of the Quran is far more serious, fierce, and tricky than that regarding Muhammad. On the outside, the announced goal is to scrutinize the Quran, similar to the way scholars scrutinized the Christian and Jewish bibles, in order to produce a so-called "critical copy".

If we were to study their goals closely, we would conclude that these scholars are "hunting" literally for pre-Uthmanic Qurans that could prove that the "real" Quran was a different book, possibly a Christian book. So now, we are told that there are two or more Qurans. In reality, these scholars are resurrecting the nineteenth-century under-accomplished theories of Reverend Alfonso Mengena, which were discarded even by most Western scholars of that time. Background: In the late 19th century, Mengena managed to get his hands on an old erased Quran manuscript from Egypt with Christian writings superimposed perpendicularly on it. He used his discovery to prove centuries old claim by some Christians that the Quran was in part a Syriac Christian book of hymns, therefore he felt enabled to question its authenticity.

Mengana's erased copy of the Quran, along with a few relatively recent copies discovered with a stash of older Qurans in the Grand Mosque of Sanaa (Yemen) and in Morocco, are the active ingredients of the current Western scholarly project to "expose" the "original" Quran. The more recent copies are part of what is referred to as the Sanaa Codex, the Munich Archive, or the Bergstraesser Archive. These copies are hailed as a possible breakthrough evidence to prove — even before examining them — that the Caliph 'Uthmān' edition of the Quran was not identical to the Quran of Muhammad.

In a second lengthy article, once again written by Andrew Higgins, the WSJ reported that a sizeable grant was awarded to German and other Western scholars to study the origins of the Quran based on these discovered and re-discovered copies. The article was titled "*The Lost archives: Missing for a half century, a cache of photos spurs sensitive research on Islam's holy text*". [2] Like a science fiction thriller, it described the re-discovery of Quranic manuscripts found "miraculously" at the Bavarian Academy of Science in Munich, Germany, where they have been missed since 1944. After stating, "Ms.

Neuwirth, a professor of Arabic studies at Berlin's Free University, is now overseeing a revival of the research [Quranic scripts];" it goes on to say, "The project renews a grand tradition of German Quranic scholarship that was interrupted by the Third Reich." Mr. Higgins' article was a series of anecdotal stories fashioned to make the "discovery" of alleged manuscripts akin to "breakthrough evidence" which may lead us to the "true" missing Quran.

The captivating details of the story reported by Higgins could be explosive ingredients, so to speak, for a suspense novel or Hollywood movie. While it seemed informative and even convincing, this story was very questionable. According to the reporter, a student and protégée of a recently passing German scholar decided to reveal that 450 microfilm rolls of Quran copies assembled before WWII to study "the evolution of the Quran" were actually stored secretly by her deceased professor in boxes, not destroyed by bombardment as previously believed. This "lost archive" or the so-called "Munich Archive" is to be instrumental for a new project —not surprisingly led by that ex-student — to produce a "critical version" of the Quran for the first time in the history of Islamic scholarship. The reporter explains: "the project, launched last year at the Berlin-Brandenburg Academy of Science and Humanities, has state funding for 18 years but could take much longer." My viewpoint: to a serious researcher, revealing the archive after 60 years of its "disappearance" and only after the passing of the professor, in the midst of a global Islamofobia environment, should be a clear indication that this project is anything but scholarly. I must add, by putting that ex-student in charge of the project with all the associated employment security and fame is, at best, seriously problematic and raises too many questions.

The reporter goes on to explain: "applying Western critical methods to Islam's holiest text is a sensitive test of the Muslim community's readiness to both accommodate and absorb thinking outside its own traditions." This statement, as we have already seen above, and will see more later on, reveals an important element shared by many Western scholars: *Critical and valid research can only be produced by Western scholarship, and that the huge amount of research and scholarly work by scholars of the Islamic Arab civilization era is irrelevant and biased.*

Ironically, the reporter complains, "modern approaches to textual analysis developed in the West are viewed in much of the Muslim world as irrelevant, at best". However, he, thankfully, admits, "Europeans started to study the Quran in the middle ages, largely in an effort to debunk it."

To transform theories about the Quran into "scholarly" facts, another group of Western scholars including a German, writing under the pseudo name Christoph Luxenburg, believe that the Quran was in part a Syriac Christian book that was translated, sometimes incorrectly, to Arabic. [4][8] Fishing out possible coincidental Syriac word combinations within historical pre-diacritics Arabic script, and exploiting a few known and expected scriptural and interpretational uncertainties in a historical reference book like the Quran, they end up formulating bizarre and contradicting linguistic alternatives. However, as we know it today, the Syriac-Aramaic language, sharing similar roots as that of old Arabic, is a poor and limited etymological reference to explain the words of the Quranic Arabic language — especially because, following Islam and the dominance of Arabic in the 7th century, this language had substantially incorporated many newer Arabic words, therefore significantly transforming itself in its fashion. Clearly, Luxenburg's work seems more like a typical Christian scholarly work than an impartial research on the history of the Quran and its language.

One must emphasize here, studying the language and history of the Quran impartially, is, of course, a very legitimate scholarly work. Indeed, a high volume of research by Muslim scholars about the Quran is abundant and it includes disagreements on word meanings, grammar, language, and history. What sets the recent trend in western scholarship aside is that it had reached predetermined conclusions before starting the research. Most important, it is deceptive. For example, some conveniently neglect to inform their readers that Muhammad had acknowledged, from the very beginning, that his message and most of the moral allegories and teachings of the Quran are closely associated with those told in Judaism and Christianity.

Regardless, should the researchers involved in this endeavor succeed to resurrect a pre-Uthmanic Quran one day, it is difficult to imagine why must we conclude that the latter and not the current Quran, was the original one as delivered by Muhammad? Even though the work by Caliph *'Uthmān* was intended to finalize chapters' names and organization of the Quran, it is a fairly known and accepted fact by all Muslim scholars — old and new — that his action came about to prevent actual attempts by some to add and delete from the original words delivered by Muhammad. In the end, finding a forged Quran would not be a valuable scholarly discovery. I must point out that, as we speak, there are those who are working very hard to distribute and promote new forged Qurans. For example, a California based group is marketing a look-alike Quran under the name: *al-Furqān*!

To answer some of the recent theories questioning the possibility of large-scale discrepancies between today's Uthmanic Quran and some earlier editions, I chose to *actually* read and compare a generous number of sample pages from the discovered Quranic manuscripts reported by Mr. Higgins article in the WSJ. As I demonstrated in the previous section, my readings proved that the current edition of the Quran is, indeed, highly accurate.

Addressing all controversial claims put forward by old and contemporary Western scholars regarding Muhammad and the Quran would be too involved and outside the scope of this book. Perhaps, the best response was the one presented by the excellent work of M.S.M. Saifulla and Abdullah David who made available online a comprehensive collection of inscriptions, manuscripts, coinage and bibliographies to aid serious and open-minded researchers and readers to examine these relevant material evidences by themselves. My research would have been extremely difficult without the valuable tools provided on their *Islamic Awareness* website. [10]

Bibliography

1. Higgins, Andrew. "The Lost Archive." *The Wall Street Journal*, January 12, 2008. http://online.wsj.com/article/SB120008793352784631.html
2. Higgins, Andrew. "Professor Hired for Outreach to Muslims Delivers a Jolt." *The Wall Street Journal*, November 15, 2008. http://online.wsj.com/article/SB122669909279629451.html http://online.wsj.com/article/SB122633888141714211.html
3. Jāsim, 'Azīz al-Sayyid. *Muḥammad: al-Ḥaqīqah al-'Uẓmá*. Baghdād: Dār al-Shu'ūn al-Thaqāfiyyah al-'Āmmah, 1987.
4. Luxenberg, Christoph. *Die Syro-Aramäische Lesart des Qur'an: Ein Beitrag zur Entschlüsselung der Qur'ansprache*. Berlin: 2000.
5. Marek, Kurt W. (C. W. Ceram). *Gods, Graves, and Scholars: the Story of Archælogy*. New York: Alfred A. Knopf, 1968. Second Edition.
6. *The Monks of Kublai Khan, the Emperor of China: The History of the Life and Travels of Rabban Sawma, Envoy and Plenipotentiary of the Mongol Khans to the Kings of Europe,*

and Markos who as Mar Yahbh-Allaha III became Patriarch of the Nestorian Church in Asia. Translated from the Syriac by Sir E. A. Wallis Budge, KT. London: The Religious Tract Society, 1928.

7. Nasser-Eddine, Minerva. "The Raging Beast Within Us All: Civil Liberties and the War on Terror." *Borderlands E-Journal* 1, no.1 (2002.) http://borderlands.net.au/vol1no1_2002/nasser_eddine.html
8. Ohlig, Karl-Heinz, and Gerd-R. Puin (Hg). *Die dunklen Anfänge: neue Forschungen zur Entstehung und frühen Geschichte des Islam.* Berlin: Verlag Hans Schiler, 2005.
9. Russell, Bertrand. *A History of Western Philosophy.* New York: Simon and Shcuster, 1945.
10. Saifullah, M. S. M, and Abdullah David. "Dated Texts Mentioning Prophet Muhammad From 1-100 AH/622-719 CE." http://www.islamic-awareness.org
11. Thomas, Lowell. *With Lawrence in Arabia.* New York: The Century Co., 1924.
12. Tschanz, D., and H. Abbas. "History's Hinge: 'Ayn Jalut." *Saudi Aramco World* 58, no. 4 (2007): 25-33.
13. al-Wardī, 'Alī. *Lamaḥat Ijtimā'iyyah min Ta'rīkh al-'Irāq al-Ḥadīth.* al-Jus' al-Awwal. Baghdād: Maṭba'at al-Irshād, 1969. First Edition.
14. Weatherford, Jack. *Genghis Khan and the Making of the Modern World.* New York: Three Rivers Press, 2004.
15. Wikipedia. "Criticism of Muhammad." http://en.wikipedia.org/wiki/Criticism_of_Muhammad

CHAPTER 2

The Arabs and Arabic Language: Evidence and Scholars

Previously, we explored a few controversial claims and theories formulated by a minority group of Western scholars, which were presented, with the help of the influential mass media, as breakthrough "scholarly facts." In this chapter, we will examine the mainstream Western theories about the history of Arabia and the Arabic language and script, as presented since the 18-19th century. Many in the Arab and Islamic worlds refer to these theories as Western theories, to distinguish them from past Islamic Arab civilization theories. Regrettably, many people today uncritically assume that these Western theories are the final verdict on a given subject, thus creating a research environment that is not only dismissive of the valuable scholarly work of past Islamic Arab era, but also of any current work referencing them. Nowadays, it became extremely difficult for researchers, whose views and conclusions are not conforming to the mainstream theories of Western scholarship in this field, to present their work or at least to be heard.

To reiterate a previous statement, a scholar needs not be of Western European extraction to subscribe to the theories of Western scholarship. Proving this point is the multitude of modern-day Arab and/or Muslim scholars who, to be accepted amidst the academic research circles, fashion their work to fit the pre-conceived guidelines provided by these circles. The famed Egyptian Arab linguist and historian, *Ṭaha Ḥusayn*, was even willing to deny the existence of pre-Islamic Arabic poetry in his Ph.D. dissertation in the Sorbonne, before reversing his position few years later. It is puzzling to see most modern-day Arab and Muslim scholarly circles pour exaggerated praise and admiration on the fascinating work made by the past Islamic Arab civilization scholars, but, at the same time, endorse and promote as "facts" Western theories that are in direct contradiction with the research and analyses made by those admired Islamic Arab scholars. A reason, therefore, exists to suspect that many modern-day Arab and Muslim researchers might not have bothered to investigate the theories presented by either side: Western or Arabic/Islamic.

In this chapter, I am going to discuss the origins of the Arabs and their language as told in the clashing theories of Western and Islamic Arab scholars. I will support my many observations through quotations from scholarly writings, old and contemporary. Additionally, I will discuss quotations from my email communications with contemporary scholars who were asked to review, anonymously, my research papers that were submitted to prominent scholarly Western publications. Most important, I will demonstrate how the main theme of modern Near East Western scholarship came about, and particularly how some of its unsubstantiated assumptions and theories are being implemented as the undisputable facts of this field.

2.1 Languages and Peoples of the Peninsula: Arabic or Semitic?

Asking the question whether the old languages of the greater Arabian Peninsula are Arabic or "Semitic" may sound confusing as much as contradictory due to the implied intent of terminology. As far as it concerns the field of Near East studies, this is the cardinal question to ask as well as to answer. For thousands of years, the Arabs proudly traced their origin to Yemen — as the home of the earliest Arab tribes. Their natural conviction is, therefore, elementary and true: If Yemen was their point of origin, it follows then that the Yemenite tongue — precisely the Arabic language — was necessarily their earliest tongue. Numerous scholars of the Islamic Arab civilization era wrote hundreds of volumes and presented countless historic facts in support of this verifiable conviction. [1] Yet, it is odd, if not perplexing, to notice how contemporary Western theories dismiss — entirely, haughtily, and arbitrarily—the magnificent work of these scholars. More perplexing, some scholars do not only dismiss that Yemen was the place of origin of the Arabs, but also advance unsubstantiated theories claiming that the Yemenis were not Arabs, that their language was not Arabic, and that the Arabs were outsiders to Yemen. They suggest that the old Yemenite language was just another "Semitic" language that "relates" to Arabic in the fashion of the Akkadian language, for example.

Yet, the word "Semitic" is only a coined term. German seminarist, historian, and philologist August Ludwig von Schlözer coined it in the 18th century to classify some languages of the Near East and North-East Africa. [8] While Schlözer intended the term to describe Middle Eastern languages with similar structure, conjugations, and vocabulary, the term itself has no contextual validity attesting to the existence of people called "Semitic" or to a language called "Semitic." It is known that Schlözer, a student of the Christian religion and a believer in the Hebrew Bible, fashioned the name given to these languages after Shem, the son of Noah in the Biblical mythology. Unfortunately, following in the footsteps of Western scholarship, even the people of the Middle East, including the Arabs, began using this invented term to describe their origin and languages. However, this is not only a paradox but also outright perversion of historical facts. For example, we know that the Latin people (and language) take their name from the region of Latium in central Italy. We also know that the word "English", used to describe a person of certain origin and specific place, owes its existence or takes its configuration from the land of "Angeln" in Germany. Further, we know that the Russian, people and languages, take their names from the old Slavic word "Rusĭl", a region in Eastern Europe (northern Ukraine, Russia, Belarus, and eastern Poland.) So, where in any geographical or inscriptional records one can find a region in the Middle East called "Shem" or language called "Shemitic"? Where can we find an area in the whole Middle East or beyond where "Semites" existed and that their language was called, "Semitic"? It stands to logic, therefore, that the use of the term "Semitic" in any context is not only a misnomer, but also a risky practice that can thwart scholars from classifying the real identity of the peoples and languages of the Middle East. If correct order is relevant to any classification, then all the languages of the old Near East should be described as *Arabic* Languages, because *all available historic, geographic and linguistic* evidence show Arabic, which was spoken by the absolute majority in the Peninsula, is what all other tongues are related to and can be derived from.

To recapitulate, *there is no one single inscriptional evidence* attesting to the existence of a group of people referred to as "Semites" living in a specific geographic and historical period, who were speaking a specific definitive independent language that we had to refer to as the "Semitic language." Now then, since this linguistic generalization is erroneous from the root, so all of its details and elaborations that some scholars built on and subsequently took for granted as the final truth about the origin of the languages in the Near East. Of course, the hypothesis of the existence of such earlier undefined, geographically and linguistically, original people and language is logically possible, but choosing the noun "Semites" and the adjective "Semitic" to describe them is obviously driven by religion and ideology, not by logic or scholarship. It is beyond our understanding, therefore, why would one ignore the facts of geography and available inscriptions to hypothesize about the existence of such people and language whereas ample evidence attests that ancient Yemen and proximate southern area was the home of such people and language. In fact, the historical and inscriptional evidence supports the theories of the earlier Muslim scholars. Today, even anthropologists believe (based on discovered evidence) that early humans migrated to Yemen coming from the Horn of Africa, which, geographically, is located on the eastern shores of Africa opposite to Yemen.

According to modern research and archeological discoveries, it is clear that many tribes of the Arabian Peninsula who spoke initially an earlier version of the Arabic language (closely related to the old Yemen language) had migrated north carrying with them their languages and dialects, which were gradually changed consequent to interactions with northern local and foreign populations. In due time, this language and dialects evolved to form either significantly different dialects now we call languages (i.e. Aramaic, Hebrew), or slightly different dialects (i.e. Nabataean and Hijazi, or the dialects of Najd and Eastern Arabia.) The most accurate, scientific and impartial term to name the family encompassing all these newly formed languages and dialects is, therefore, Arabic. Even T. E. Lawrence, with his extreme deArabization mindset, has observed this Arabic language classification terminology. [6]

Arabs who did not migrate north continued using the old Arabic language (including Sabaian and Himyarite) relatively unchanged before and after Islam. Many parallel examples upholding this hypothesis exist. Among these is the language of the Saxon Germanic people who migrated to the British Island to become what is known today as the English language, or the Anglo-Saxon and Dutch European language mixture in South Africa that eventually became the Afrikaans. Based on this argument, is it permissible to hypothesize that the English people were a distinct group of people living in mainland Europe and speaking the English language, old or new, before migrating to the British Island? The answer should be no, unless one can provide a cogent explanation.

Two facts upheld by geography, geology, and archeology endorse the theories of Islamic Arab era scholars. First, thousands of years before the Christian era, the vast Arabian Peninsula was much greener and more populated, but consequent to continuous desertification and famine (similar to what is happening in Africa today) it became the main source for repeated waves of population migrations toward the fertile lands situated further north. Attesting to this fact is the Sumerian city of Ur, which was founded adjacent to the Euphrates River and to the nearby gulf (the Arabian-Persian Gulf today.)

Today, Ur sits in the middle of the desert. Second, based on historical research and records obtained from thousands of discovered Musnad inscriptions, the Arabic language, with all its flavors and dialects, was (for thousands of years before the advent of Islam) the language of the absolute majority of population of the Arabian Peninsula, south and north.

A key element that distinguishes Western theories is their definition of the terms "Arab" and "Arabic." One constantly reads that if the people of old Yemen were Arabs, why did not they say so in the numerous Yemeni Musnad inscriptions found today. Others like to over-emphasize that the earliest discovered evidence mentioning the word "Arab" was the Monolith inscription of Shalmaneser II, which was recorded in the Akkadian language of Mesopotamia and is dated back to the 9th century BCE. The amazement does not stop here; many Western scholars approximate the existence of the Arabs and their language to that timeframe. That is to only a nine hundred years before the Christian Calendar as if the Arabs were some sort of a sudden germination.

Today, it is highly instructive to notice how inaccuracies mingle with academic studies in the field of Arabic philology and etymology. A website called "etymonline.com" is a classic example of extreme scientific banality when it comes to defining the word Arab:

> Arab (n.) Late 14c. (Arabiens), from O.Fr. Arabe, from L. Arabs (acc. Arabem), from Gk. Araps (gen. Arabos), from Ar-

> abic 'arab, indigenous name of the people, perhaps lit. "inhabitant of the desert" (rel. to Heb. arabha "desert"). Meaning "homeless little wanderer, child of the street" is from 1848, in ref. to nomadic ways." [4]

As one can see, the above was not a serious research in etymology, but a clear piece of naïve terminology where the Arabs, the progenitors of most peoples of the Arabian Peninsula became defined in terms of the Hebrew dialect, and where the word "Arab" is taking its sound from the assumingly Hebrew word, "arabha"...

To conclude, the mortal flaw in the mainstream Western theories dealing with the history and origin of the Arabs and Arabic language is this: peoples and civilizations do not necessarily refer to themselves using terms invented or adopted by others — the dubbing of the Original Peoples of the Americas as "Indians" is a classic example. To illustrate this situation consider the following: the ancient Athenians used the term "Barbarian" to call any one who was not Athenian. However, it has never been recorded that those whom Athens called "Barbarians" had ever dubbed, referred to, or called themselves as such. Further, given the deeply rooted tribal nature of the Arabs, they have historically used their tribal identity —precisely, the identity of the ruling tribe — rather than their ethnic one. Following in this tradition, they usually identify themselves as *Nazār*, *Ma'ad*, *Abbāsiyīns*, *Umawiyyīn*, etc. These were the namesakes of tribal leaders and rulers. Even today, an Arab from the heartland of the Arabian Peninsula (Saudi Arabia) would (unfortunately) refer to himself or herself as Saudi, which is the clan name of the ruling family!

Before Islam, the word Arab was used mainly to refer to blood ties and ethnical purity. In modern-day Iraq where this author, an ethnically Arab, was raised, Arabs who settled in cities (whether only decades or centuries ago) would refer to populations of the surrounding countryside and deserts as "the Arabs." This old practice clearly alludes to these people's ethnic purity supposedly evident by their unwillingness to intermarry outside their tribes.

After the advent of Islam, which fought tribalism and ethnic chauvinism, the spoken language gradually substituted ethnic purity as the main factor to classify who is an Arab. An Arab became anyone with a native Arabic tongue, *of any dialect*, and upbringing. This tradition has continued through the present age. The pre-Islamic inscription of *al-Namārah*, dated 328 CE, which we will study in details in Chapter 4, is an excellent evidence to back this conclusion. It used the term "*king of all Arabs*," to refer to authentic Arabs, but called ethnically mixed Arabs by their tribal identity or names. Incidentally, the use of the word "*all*" in that inscription is very significant. It clearly indicates that the term "Arabs" was referring to a vast diverse group of ethnically and culturally homogenous people living in a large geographical location that contained the majority of their population, regardless of distribution, in the Arabian Peninsula. By logic and common sense, this geographical location cannot be but the heart of the Fertile Crescent where this king had ruled from (*al-Hīrah*, 50 miles south of Babylon) and where this inscription was found (Damascus)!

In fact, according to *al-Fihrast* of *Ibn al-Nadīm* (929 - 996 CE,) a well-known historian and librarian living in Baghdad during the times of the Abbasid Caliphate, it was a common believe then that the Nabataean language was the old language of Babylon and that the Chaldeans (*al-Kildāniyyūn*) and Assyrians (*al-Siryāniyyūn*) spoke varied dialects of it. [9] Observing that the Nabataean language is substantially Arabic — as clearly seen in modern-day inscriptions — this would endorse the notion put forward throughout this book, that old Arabic was the root of the Near East languages, and that Arabic, not Aramaic, was the predominant tongue of most of the Fertile Crescent, before Islam.

Misnaming the absolute majority and original people of Arabia as "Semites" would therefore deprive the Arabs from their natural self-denomination. This term, as explained earlier, is not a term found in the inscriptions, but invented in the 18th century to describe affinities among the languages and dialects, old or new, of the Near East. Strangely enough, the same scholars *who uphold the existence of the never-existed "Semites" demand inscriptional evidence to validate the Arabs' assertion that they are Arabs!* To deflate the whole affair, suffice to say that in terms of validity and unlike the term "Semites" that appeared nowhere in any historical world prior to 1786 when Schlözer coined it, the term "Arabs" at least existed. Not only did it exist, but was also used in actual inscriptions where it referred to the populations in and south of the Fertile Crescent many centuries before the Christian era.

M.C.A. MacDonald, a preeminent Western expert of the Arabic language, accredited for his detailed study on the languages of old Arabia, is a good example of how today's academic circles employ odd language classifications of pre-Islamic Arabia that in effect *de-Arabize* Arabia and the Arabs. [7] MacDonald felt free to dismantle the old Arabic language and reclassify local dialects into tens of confusing independent languages linked by their "Semitic" roots. In effect, in employing such method, MacDonald eliminated all historical roots of the Arabic language as it was recorded in the pre-Islamic poetry, as well as in the Quran. Regarding Yemen, for example, he wrote, "neither the Ancient nor the Modern South Arabian languages are in any sense 'Arabic'." He observed: "The presence of *al* in a name does not mean that the text in which the name occurs is in Old Arabic."

To debate MacDonald's view, this could be true *only* if one is dealing with a non-Arabic text (Greek, for example), not a text filled with many other words that are clearly Arabic. MacDonald goes further in his highly unsubstantiated analysis by hinting that even Arabic dialects like Thamudic, Lihyanic, and Safaitic, are not Arabic. This brings us to wonder, if he also believes that the Ummuwayites and the Abasiddes spoke different languages after the advent of Islam!

Full sub-classification of a language based on dialectical flavors is an important and legitimate scholarly work, especially if these flavors belong to one language. Despite many useful scholarly classifications presented in MacDonald's comprehensive linguistic map study, his one-sided scholarly vision is immediately noticeable from reading the first pages. Thus, based on personal opinion and without any historical proof whatsoever, he writes, "Old Arabic was a minority language in the Arabian Peninsula and only became the Arabic language for the majority after Islam".

However, MacDonald's statement above, which summarizes the theme of Western scholarship on the history of the Arabic language, is not only inaccurate and opinionated, but is also misleading. Even though the Muslim Arabs may have imposed their new religion on the pagan majority of Arabia, through protection and tax incentives, their old Arabic language and its closely related derived dialects were already dominant in the Arabian Peninsula, Fertile Crescent, and the North and Horn of Africa. Structurally, old Arabic was the root tongue to Aramaic, Nabataean, Babylonian, Mandaic, Hebrew, Phoenician, and other evolved dialects. It is quite evident that the Muslim Arabs of *Ḥijāz* were at home in Iraq, Syria, Palestine, and Egypt, and had assimilated easily and rapidly with the vast majority of the populations in these neighboring territories.

Some Western scholars are more creative in incorporating the "Semitic" theory in the body of their research while persistently ignoring past Islamic Arab scholarship. Thomas Thompson, the author of *Mythic Past*, is such a scholar. [11] Even though he authored progressive essays on the mythical nature of the stories narrated in the Bible, he, after visiting Israel and after meeting strong objections on his earlier work, greatly contradicted himself. He resorted to the use of the term "Semitic" to name the peoples of the Near East, even though such term is void of any historical validity. In his work, which effectively de-roots the Arabs from Arabia, Thompson delves into groundless historical speculations by ascribing the origins of the Arabs to North Africa. So, in order for us to discover the origins of these "mysterious" Arabs and their language, he recommends that we need to "go far back to the North African ancestors of the speakers of Semitic languages".

Thompson further explains how "They lived in the Green Sahara until late in the seventh Millennium BCE when a long and relentless drought" forced them east "and finally, crossing the Nile, to Palestine by way of the Sinai." According to Thompson, the proto-Semitic people who settled in Palestine —Israel today — are the original "Semitic speakers of Asia". To explain the roots of the "Semites," Thompson used the same speculative and theoretical underpinnings of the current theory of Western scholarship: the northern Semites were migrants from a drought stricken area [sic]. The only difference that Thompson makes here is that he exchanges the Arabian Desert with the African Sahara.

One does not need to dissect Thompson words — they speak for themselves — to uncover the irrationality of the assumption he presented, the unsubstantiated accounts he told, the historical theorizations he embarked on, and, of course, the inconsistency of his conclusions. As he improvised himself as sure seer of what happened 7000 years before Christ, he also demonstrated how unrepresentative scholarly work could lead to cute stories fashioned as scientific data.

Another (very) curious point: Thompson does not explain why an ancient relentless drought was only possible in the African Sahara but not in the vast Arabian desert, especially when we have archeological evidence of buried cities even in the "Empty Quarter" of Arabia? Nor does he offer any compelling evidence that the "Semitic" people of North African were the original ones. He explains how the ancestors of the "Semites" were inhabitants of "a village culture of farmers and shepherds", but he fails to explain why these African proto-Semites would decide to cross the Sinai desert rather than settling fully around the Niles or fertile Palestine! He did not even bother to explain his strange theory of migration especially in the part where some of these proto-Semites decided (after being accustomed to an agricultural life) to start roaming the vast Arabian Desert to became Arab nomads (Bedouins). If common sense matters, it is statistically impossible that a subset of these proto-Semitic African farmers would turn into Arab Bedouins, who were by far the largest "Semitic" population in the Peninsula. In reality, the trend was (and still is) unidirectional; that is, the Bedouins would gradually settle to create urban centers, not the reverse.

Like many other Western scholars, Thompson dug himself into the notion that the Arabs are the Bedouins of the Arabian Desert. But had he consulted a dictionary of the Arabic language, he would have learned that the word Bedouins (Arabic: *al-Badawiyyūn*), is associated with the word *Bādiyah*, which means "desert plains." Thus, Bedouins means the dwellers of the *Bādiyah* as distinct from the same people who live in population centers that the Arabs normally refer to as *Ḥaḍar*, meaning urbanized, that is, living in urban centers. He thinks it is not possible that those who lived and created culture in the countless population centers of the Peninsula (Petra for example) can be Arabs who became new distinctive groups later. After all, going from the mobility of hunting to the stability of settlement is the trend of human historical development, not the reverse.

As we shall see in the next section, many contemporary Western scholars would easily loose temper and even ridicule the notion that these Arab Bedouins can be the original "Semites". Indeed, Thompson loudly declares, "the earliest speakers could hardly have been Arabia's Bedouins." Such possibility according to him would be "A far cry from the old romantic fantasy of the origin of the Semites from dashing desert Bedouin tribes." However, he seems to struggle when explaining the obvious linguistic evidence built in the Arabic language, which incontrovertibly indicates that Arabic was the mother root of all other "Semitic" languages. He admits, "Arabic seemed earlier because so much of its grammar has preserved antique forms." He also admits, "Arabic, Akkadian, and the West Semitic languages have a common vocabulary for words related to agriculture, horticulture, and herding," which are, to our knowledge, the bulk of vocabulary forming any typical historical language. Adding some archeological justification to his theory that the people of the Levant (particularly the population of Palestine) were the original Asian Semites, Thompson explains: "As Mesopotamia had only a very short period of pre-Bronze Age settlement, Syria and Palestine became the most promising area for the earliest development of the Semitic language." The question remains, where did Thompson get such lopsided information from? Does he not know that archeologists and anthropologists had found fossils of Homo erectus in northern Mesopotamia that predates those found in Palestine?

Thompson's bizarre and unsubstantiated theories regarding the "Semites" and Arabs are not unique. Another Western scholar, Jan Retsö, who published a recent book dedicated to the history of the Arabs, "*The Arabs in antiquity: their history from the Assyrians to the Umayyads*," went even further in his weird theorizations. [10] While Thompson theorized about the origins of the Arabs indirectly as another "Semite" group, Retsö singled them out specifically. In his book, Retsö did not only subscribe to the theme of established scholarly theories postulating that the Arabs are the youngest group in the Arabian Peninsula who appeared, *somehow*, in the 9th century BCE (the date of the *earliest found* inscription mentioning the word Arab), but he expanded much further to "prove" it. According to Retsö, the Arabs were not even a nation or an original ethnic group, but a religious community. (We will come back to Retsö in the next section.) For now though, to best summarize his theorizations about the Arabs and their history, I will borrow from Google Books' summary of Retsö's book without any elaboration:

> "This book describes the history of the Arabs in antiquity from their earliest appearance around 853 BC until the first century of Islam. It traces the mention of people called Arabs in all relevant ancient sources and suggests a new interpretation of their history. It is suggested that the ancient Arabs were more a religious community than an ethnic group, which would explain why the designation 'Arab' could be easily adopted by the early Muslim tribes. The Arabs of antiquity thus resemble the early Islamic Arabs more than is usually assumed, both being united by common bonds of religious ideology and law."

Without a doubt, language is the most important and defining factor to classify a group of people, like the Arabs. Studying the origins of a language would necessarily highlight the origins of its speakers. In my view, which conforms with the core view of early Islamic Arab era scholars, there is a good reason to believe that southern Arabian *Sab'ic* or northern Arabian Nabataean and Akkadian, for example, are as substantially linked to Arabic as many other modern and old Arabic language dialects. That is, classic (or standard) Arabic is the best available tool to read inscriptions of the old languages of the greater Arabian Peninsula, correctly.

To support my argument, above, it is important to read what paramount Muslim Arab scholar and philosopher *Ibn Khaldūn* wrote more than a thousand-year ago: "The *Ḥimīr* language is another language that differs from the *Muḍar* language in many of its derivations and vocalizations aspects, the same way our current Arabic language differs from the *Muḍar* language." [2] Like other Islamic Arab era scholars of his time, *Ibn Khaldūn* used the word "language" clearly in the meaning of "tongue" or "dialect." His statement plainly classified the old Yemen language, which he called the "*Ḥimīr* language," as an Arabic language that differed from the Arabic language of the early years of Islam, which he called the "*Muḍar* language," the same way the Arabic language of his days (centuries after Islam) differed from the "*Muḍar* language."

The fact that the Arabs had treated derived and related Arabic languages in the region as just dialects or "tongues" is quite evident in the Quran. For example, in *Sūrat al-Naḥl* (16:103), the Quran tells us that the person who conversed with Prophet Muhammad (a Christian priest named *Baḥira* according to most history sources) spoke with *lisānun A'jamī* or "non-Arabic tongue." The Arabs used the term "*lisanun 'Arabī*" in the meaning of pure, formal, or classic Arabic, as recorded in the Quran. This was their reference tongue to compare all other derived and related Arabic tongues in the region with, including that of the population centers of Hijaz. In *Sūrat al-Qiṣaṣ* (88:34) the Quran used أَفْصَحُ مِنِّي لِسانًا, in the meaning of "the one with more formal or classic tongue." Clearly, it was not referring to a different or independent language.

Above all, the undisputed evidence supporting our classification of these languages as essentially Arabic is etched on the thousands of Musnad inscriptions discovered in modern times. I said undisputed because of one simple fact: *no one can read these inscriptions correctly without utilizing classic Arabic linguistic tools.* Classic, Standard, or Formal Arabic should not be classified, therefore, as a separate language that was actually spoken by any particular group in Arabia, but rather as the "pure" or "root" of the Arabic language itself. In other words, Classic Arabic is the formal grammatical reference of the original Arabic language. Even before Islam, only a very small minority spoke with classic Arabic tongue, especially in the population centers. Many sent their sons to live with Arab tribes around cities to acquire "pure" Arabic linguistic skills. It was told that even Prophet Muhammad was sent in the desert outside of Mecca to acquire Arabic linguistic purity.

At this point, rather than keep speculating on this topic, it would be more useful that we study the evidence of some typical sample inscriptions. In chapters 3 and 4, I will read important Nabataean inscriptions from northern Arabia and a typical Musnad inscription from southern Arabia, Yemen. In addition to preparing the readers for chapter 5 which deals with the history of modern Arabic script, my in-depth examination of these inscriptions could also help them explore, on their own, the roots of the Arabic language by inspecting typical pre-Islamic linguistic environments of two greatly separated geo-historical locations of the Arabian Peninsula.

My reading of the inscriptions utilizing classic Arabic, primarily, and employing the historical frameworks specified by theories put forward by accomplished scholars of the Islamic Arab Civilization era, is crucial in one specific regard — it gives the necessary resources to challenge the claims that contemporary Western scholarship formulates about the history of the Arabic language. This is particularly important, especially considering the magnitude of fundamental errors that many contemporary scholars committed when reading inscriptions utilizing all but the vital Arabic linguistic tools to justify their visions and conclusions.

In spite of my conviction, I believe that reading inscriptions should not be the only method to study the history of languages and scripts. It is expected that scholars should choose to be analytical and take into accounts all previously accumulated knowledge, including the specific knowledge that was transferred to us via religion and popular narratives. However, I definitely share the modern Western scholarship opinion that considers the inscriptions as paramount evidence.

Nevertheless, it would be reasonable to assert that reading an inscription should never be considered final and that repeated verifications are required to determine validity. Beyond that, I strongly suggest that students and readers of the history of Arabic script and language should not take experts' claims for granted. All important evidence should be examined personally to evaluate the tools and assumptions that previous scholars used to reach their conclusions.

2.2 The Peer Review Process of Near East Scholarship

Before proceeding to the actual readings of relevant inscriptions, it is of great research value to share with the readers my experiences with five major Near East Western scholarly journals. The quotes from email correspondences presented in this section will directly illustrate the theme and vision advocated by the contemporary Western scholarly theories regarding the history of Arabia and the Arabic language and script. They are clear material evidence to explain in details how these theories are maintained as the mainstream facts of this highly complex and debated field. Since presenting modern scholarly theories alone is not sufficient to establish them as scientific facts, and wanting validate them nevertheless, some Western scholarly circles seem to resort to censorship to accomplish the task, by invoking a "double-edged" selective process known as the "scholarly peer-review" process. It is a fact that this imperfect process can easily be abused and even turned into a tool for "scholarly Censorship."

While the peer-review process is, undoubtedly, an important avenue to evaluate studies and research papers to determine fitness for publication — especially in a prestigious journal — this process is not without flaws, loopholes, and motivated decision-making. It is customary that in this process a reviewer or referee should primarily evaluate the quality of research and methodology employed by an author, not to agree or disagree with the conclusions and opinions presented in a paper. Furthermore, it is a matter of established professionalism that a referee's opinion is only a recommendation, *not* a precondition for publication. Since the peer-review process can be misused, editors should have the authority and obligation to correct such abuses. It is also important that serious research journals allow authors to reply to anonymous reviewers so that an editor can make a fair decision whether to proceed with the publication to the benefit of the scientific community. In my personal experience in other fields, I had papers published by Western journals even when reviewers did not recommend them. Accordingly, I have to say this: If preventive adherence to or a priori accepting of specific views and established theories were condition for agreeing to publish new perspectives on a topic, *we would have never advanced in any field.*

Since I used the term "scholarly abuse" to describe the attitude of some specialized academic research bodies versus any independent research having to deal with the subject of Arabia and the Arabic language and script, it would be useful to give practical examples. If analyzed based on its mechanism, this attitude would amount to nothing less than precise guidelines for the censorship and rejection of any conclusion that contradicts the theories of the establishment.

Following more than a year and a half of research and of reading important inscriptions, I presented my findings in two articles (integrated after minor changes in this book as Chapters 3 and 4.) The first article presented new readings of two major Nabataean inscriptions; the other presented a first-time original reading of a typical Musnad inscription from Yemen. I chose four known Western scholarly journals to publish our findings. Three journals among the roaster are *Journal of the American Oriental Society* (JAOS), *Journal of Near Eastern Studies* (JNES), and *Journal of Semitic Studies* (JSS). They have been publishing for more than a century. The forth, *Arabian Archaeology and Epigraphy* (AAE) is new, but very active, publication in the field.

To say the least, it was not surprising that all four journals swiftly rejected both articles despite the valuable new findings and the strong evidence I presented in connection with my reading of the inscriptions. Their predicted response does not end here: the editors and reviewers of the articles shared the same frankness, directness, and determination to reject dissenting voices without regard to scholarship.

To be fair, these same four journals have contributed greatly to scholarship in all fields of Near East Studies, including Arabic and Islamic studies. It is evident though, when the topic of study is about the Arabs and Arabic language and script, editors and referees of these journals patently follow pre-ordained conclusions even if they contradict with findings of authentic research. It is by weight of reasonable evidence that we declare that these conclusions constitutes and are the nucleus of a pre-established vision. As such, this vision is the principle rationale for censorship.

How did I reach this conclusion? One of the inscriptions I read, the Musnad inscription, clearly and by any account carries an Arabic text. Yet, the editors and reviewers of one of the above-mentioned journals implicitly suggested *that I do not call it Arabic text as a condition for publication ...*

Further, aside from a few notes about some details of my reading, the editors and reviewers directed their intense objection to my introductory statements and conclusions. And, all four journals distinctly appeared as inter-sharing the same primary objection: that I have suggested that *the language used in the inscriptions should be classified as Arabic; or, at most, old Arabic or special dialect of Arabic, and that classic Arabic is the common denominator required to read them.* After all, I used classic Arabic tools to read the inscriptions! The following are some of the replies from these journals: [3]

Journal of Near Eastern Studies (JNES)

> South Arabian inscriptions make it abundantly clear that the Arabs were outsiders, and that the inhabitants of Saba,

> Hadramaut, Qataban and Ma'in (not one Yemeni kingdom at this time!) and later of Himyar were not themselves Arabs ... Modern Arab nationalist perceptions suffuse this paper

Arabian Archaeology and Epigraphy (AAE)

> The interpretation you have given of the inscription is simply incorrect, because you have read it as though it were Arabic rather than Sabaic. The two languages are simply not the same....The Sabaic language, as well as the other Ancient South Arabian (ASA) languages, has nothing to do with (Classical) Arabic - apart from their historical relationship within the Semitic language family.

Journal of the American Oriental Society (JAOS)

> You apply cultural, linguistic, historiographical, and ethnological principles and presuppositions appropriate--perhaps--to the 4th-6th century A.H. to the 3rd-4th century A.D.

Journal of Semitic Studies (JSS)

> I noted also your claim that the Musnad inscriptions are in fact in Arabic ... The referee felt that the article showed inadequate background knowledge of Semitic philology and ancient South Arabian history and society.

A careful reading of these replies reveals a common standpoint: all journals, directly and indirectly, objected angrily, uniformly, and methodically to the fact that I dared to challenge the conclusions of the Near East scholarship establishment. In other words, I crossed over a red line that should have never been violated.

There is more to understand from these swift objections. Convincing evidence suggests that once the Western scholars of the 19th century challenged and replaced (without being challenged, of course) the diligent work that the scholars of the past Islamic Arab civilization era developed and completed centuries earlier, with their own theories and conclusions, a groundless "ruling" came into existence. According to this "ruling", *Western theories are verified facts; as such, they should forever remain the immutable basis for the study of the history of people and languages in the Near East.* Consequently, a closed-minded attitude developed whereby revisions, no matter how justified or required are treated with immediate rejection under the pretext for not being scholarly enough to be accepted [sic]. Overtime, this predetermined attitude became a rigid dogma that no one should challenge, change, or amend — even if warranted by updated research.

One reply — important to mention because of its clarity and critical implications — is the one we received from AAE reviewer. The reviewer complained that we dared "To reverse 100 years of scholarly work." Is it not amazing that the reviewer complained about our reversing of one hundred years of Western scholarly work while he and many of his colleagues, have reversed one thousand years of the esteemed scholarly work of the Islamic Arab civilization era?

At least two journals made the effort to remind us that even modern Arab scholars support their views. From the viewpoint of academic research, this is not bewildering but unsettling. Is "endorsement" of theories sufficient to void the clear evidence presented by the inscriptions! If this was so, then what happened to scientific research? The reply I received from JNES reviewer was remarkably arrogant. It hinted that I have crossed the established scholarly line and that I should rethink and rewrite the article in a way it can be heard. And more, after emphasizing the "many interesting small insights" and "some good ideas scattered across", the reviewer lost temper after reading my take on the history of Arabic script (the conclusion of Chapter 5.) He started "virtually shouting" using phrases that habitually do not belong to scholarly setting such as "It is totally impossible;" "The only other possibility;" and "There really is almost no point of similarity between..." The following are more quotes from theses journals' replies:

Journal of Near Eastern Studies (JNES)

> Though there are many interesting small insights in this paper, there are a few flaws so fundamental that publication would not be possible without total rethinking and rewriting...I do not think it is worth me dealing with the minor details until these major issues are addressed, but I would like to re-emphasize that there are some good ideas scattered across these pages...It is totally impossible that the Arabic script (not language) be derived from the South Arabian

> script (musnad); the only other possibility is Syriac. There really is almost no point of similarity between South Arabian script and Arabic script.

Arabian Archaeology and Epigraphy (AAE)

> If you want to publish the inscription, I would suggest that you collaborate with a trained Sabaist... Interpreting a clearly Sabaic inscription as an Arabic text means to ignore more than hundred years of scholarly work on ASA languages and epigraphy...If you wish to consult an Arab scholar, may I suggest ...

Journal of the American Oriental Society (JAOS)

> It could be a case of both having trouble with unorthodox ideas, which is not unheard of. We are a fairly atypical journal and a conservative one at that;

Journal of Semitic Studies (JSS)

> The article is unlikely to be accepted without being accompanied by a full scholarly apparatus...As you know, this is contrary to the view of the experts in Epigraphic South Arabian (including Muslim experts fully aware of early Islamic traditions, of whom there are many in Yemen and Saudi Arabia)

I must admit that a couple of reviewers did offer useful notes concerning some details of our inscriptions' readings. We took these notes seriously and addressed them accordingly. Having said that, we still want to underline that all reviewers were unambiguous about the reason why they did not recommend publication: *we dared to question established Western theories about the origins of the Arabs and the Arabic language and script.*

To summarize my viewpoint regarding the issue of publishing articles that re-opens the debate on the Arabic language and script, we pose the following questions: are we to surmise that the academic establishment of the Near East studies consider that fundamentally different conclusions reached by outsiders to its cadre of compliant scholars as being unscholarly, radical, or unorthodox? Are we to conclude that evidence gathered from the inscriptions is no longer important to Western scholars and specialized journals? In the end, suppose that I read an inscription as if it were Arabic, then turn around and state that what I read was not Arabic; would peer reviewers raise objections? Based on the preceding arguments, it is inescapable to conclude that pre-agreement with the established theories seems to be the condition for academic acceptance.

To be fair to the four journals above, I need to mention that my article was also rejected, even more swiftly (less than two weeks,) by a fifth journal: *Journal of Arabic and Islamic Studies (JAIS).* After informing me that they agree with the other four journals that my "article contains some interesting ideas," but "Its overall form and content is marred by a number of factual flaws (including transcription and comparative Semitic data,)", they complained that I "have not taken into consideration important recent studies" conducted by Retsö. In other words, their objection (declaration) can be explained as follows: researchers like myself, have to forgo their genuine findings and conclusions — no matter how substantiated and original — and subscribe as alternative to the theories they endorse — no matter how unsubstantiated or weird. Let's read their hasty reply:

Journal of Arabic and Islamic Studies (JAIS)

> What is more, you have not taken into consideration important recent studies on the an-Namara inscription, such as Jan Retsö's relevant chapter in _The Arabs in Antiquity_., where also other more recent studies on the subject are dealt with."

For the record, Retsö has not re-traced or re-read *al-Namārah* or any of the inscriptions in question. My article (Chapter 3 of this book) on the other hand, was primarily a new detailed tracing and reading of the *al-Namārah* and *Umm al-Jimāl* inscriptions. As I stated earlier, Retsö's book was primarily a history textbook with unsubstantiated theories packed as "scholarly facts." In his book, he labored to "prove" that the Arabs are not even an ethnic group, but a religious group. In the chapter mentioning the *al-Namārah* and *Umm al-Jimāl* inscriptions, Retsö did not question their established Western tracings or readings. He discussed their contents as referential facts. His main complaint was that some (like this author) have dared to reference them independently to confirm the validity of the theories put earlier by known scholars of the Islamic Arab civilization era. In other words, he discussed the content of the inscriptions only to downplay their significance as history references. Referring to the work of the great Muslim Arab historian and scholar, *al-Ṭabarī*, he complained in pages 482-485 about the "the assumption that al-Tabari and his colleagues somehow tell the correct story and that the Namara inscription should be inserted into it." [10]

It seems evident that the decision of JAIS to reject my article was solely due to their objection to the brief introductory section of the article, which, in addition to questioning the accuracy of some established Western tracings and readings of relevant inscriptions, had also included a historical review heavily referencing past scholarly work of the Arab Islamic era. Meaning, they rejected the article because it had crossed a pre-established line of reasoning. Still, the only difference between their rejection and that of the other four journals is that, apparently, the reviewer of JAIS did not even have the scholarly curiosity to read the sections detailing our re-tracing and re-reading of the inscriptions in question (56 out of 60 pages!). He simply quit after reading the first four introductory pages!

It should be pointed out that my recent experience with peer reviewers of these prominent Western Journals is not an isolated incidence or an exception. It is the norm. For example, a few years ago, a scholar from the State University of California, Alan Kaye, wrote a review in the *Journal of Near East Studies (JNES)* about a book titled "*The Origin and Evolution of Ancient Arabian Scripts"* by Majeed Khan. [5] The book is based primarily on Khan's Ph.D. thesis completed in England in 1988. In his book, Khan challenged the established Western theories on the origin of the Arabic Musnad Script. Khan, sure of his methodical research, concluded that the Musnad *Thamūdī* script was independently developed in the Arabian Peninsula. As expected, such conclusion was contrary to these theories claiming that Musnad was a proto-Sinaic script imported from the North via the Sinai Peninsula. The implication made by Khan's research was extraordinary — removing the proto-Sinaic connection could open the realistic possibility that Phoenician and Aramaic themselves are Musnad derivatives. For the record (as we shall see in Chapter 6), although there are prominent scholars who believed in such possibility, the book reviewer, Alan Kaye, felt entitled to unleash a volley of personal attacks, insults, and accusations against the researcher. He even questioned Mr. Khan's integrity by sarcastically asking: "Is it not transparent that this monograph, published by governmental agencies of Saudi Arabia, authored by a researcher employed by one of the Kingdom agencies (the Department of Antiques and Museums) should postulate that writing was invented by the Bedouins of (Saudi) Arabia?" I am tempted, myself, to ask Mr. Kaye, an employee of the California State University, a public *governmental* agency financed by state and federal governments, a similar question: Would he question any CSU publication authored by his fellow public employees regarding the history of California and the US, in the same way he did with Mr. Khan's book?

On a serious note, given the similarities between the *Thamūdī* Musnad and proto-Sinaic shapes, we do not see why it would only be possible that the primitive shapes of proto-Sinaic could be the original, albeit not those of primitive *Thamūdī*, abundantly found in the larger adjacent Arabian desert areas. It would also be appropriate to question why the reviewer have sarcastically dismissed the notion of a central role that the Bedouins of the Arabian Peninsula desert might have had in inventing or transporting Musnad, but not the notion of a central role that the Bedouins of the Sinai Peninsula desert might had in inventing or transporting proto-Sinaic! Is it because the Sinai desert played central role in Biblical mythology? The reviewer continued his asymmetrical review by saying that the study in Khan's book was "an excellent example of a politically influenced statement, with all of its nationalistic underpinnings." Does not that sound similar to the answer we got above from two of the reviewers of our work?

Another aspect we need to address, at least in passing, is the seemingly ready attack against the linguistic aspects of any book or article that does not conform to the premises of the established theories. In the case of Mr. Khan's book, the reviewer made sure to attack his English writing style. He wrote, "Level of English was not good", and that the "book was boring." To draw a parallel, two of the peer reviewers who reviewed my articles complained about the same issue — the quality of the written English used in the writing of the articles. One reviewer even suggested that I should re-write my article completely before submitting for consideration. It seems that ridiculing the work of those who dare to challenge established Western theories about the Arabic script and language has become the preferred method to escape discussing serious issues, hence to prepare the ground for rejection.

Next, I shall present my in-depth readings of relevant inscriptions — as originally included in my rejected articles mentioned above. Note: to facilitate the harmony and reading fluidity of this book, I have removed some of the introductory notes and conclusions stated elsewhere and re-wrote a few paragraphs, but kept the tracings, readings, and necessary background notes as submitted. After reading Chapter 3 and 4, I am asking the readers to decide for themselves whether to classify the inscriptional texts I read in the two chapters as essentially classic Arabic — as widely documented by pre-Islamic poems and the Quran — or as a sister "Semitic" language that is fundamentally different — as Western theories claim today.

Bibliography

1. ʿAlī, Jawād. *Tarīkh al-ʿArab qabla al-Islam*. Baghdad: al-Mujammaʿ al-ʿIlmī al-ʿIrāqī, 1959.
2. Ibn Khaldūn. *Taʾrīkh Ibn Khaldūn.* Part 1, Chapter 47.
   ابن خلدون. تأريخ ابن خلدون. الجزء الاول. الفصل 47
   http://al-eman.com/IslamLib/viewchp.asp?BID=163&CID=42

3. Email exchanges between the author and JAOS (June 2009), AAE and JSS (September 2009,) JNES (February 2010,) and JAIS (February 2011.)
4. Etymology Online. Website Entry. http://www.etymonline.com/index.php?search=arab&search-mode=none
5. Kaye, Alan. Review of *The Origin and Evolution of Ancient Arabian Scripts*, by Majeed Khan. *Journal of Near East Studies* 59, no. 3 (July 2000): 213-214.
6. Lawrence, T. E. *Seven Pillars of Wisdom: a Triumph.* New York: Doubleday, Doran & Company Inc, 1936.
7. MacDonald, M. C. A. "Reflections on the Linguistic map of Pre-Islamic Arabia." Arabian *Archeology and Epigraphy* 11 (2000): 28-79.
8. Mahdī, Sāmī. "Aqwām al-Jazīrah al-'Arabiyyah wa Ūsūlahā." *Al-Quds al-'Arabi Newspaper,* October 5, 2009, Online Edition.
9. al-Nadīm, Ibn. *The Fihrest of al-Nadim.* Translated and Edited by Bayard Dodge. New York: Columbia University Press, 1970.
10. Retsö, Jan. *The Arabs in antiquity: their history from the Assyrians to the Umayyads.* London; New York: Routledge Curzon, 2003.
11. Thompson, Thomas L. *The Mythic Past: Biblical Archeology and the Myth of Israel.* New York: Basic Books, 1999.

CHAPTER 3

The *al-Namārah* Nabataean Arabic Inscription (328 CE)

3.1 Introduction

The inscription of *al-Namārah* is by far the most important, controversial, and challenging pre-Islamic Arabic inscription—it is the earliest discovered but youngest dated inscription of only three Nabataean inscriptions considered by Western scholars today as fully Arabic. It is also the oldest Arabic document on record with relatively good classic Arabic language. Dated 328 AD and written in clear cursive forms, it was hailed by many scholars as definite evidence that the modern Arabic script had evolved from the late Nabataean script. Many prominent Muslim scholars (who lived only a few centuries after the script's assumed birth around the 3rd century) believed it was derived from the Arabic *Musnad* script. *al-*

Namārah inscription is also extensively cited by historians as an important reference to the historical events of the early decades of the prominent pre-Islamic Arab Lakhmid kingdom (*al-Lakhmiyyūn*) of *Hīrah*, modern day Iraq. Despite more than a century since its discovery in 1901, the reading of *al-Namārah* inscription is still questionable, even at present time.

Dussaud, the French archeologist who discovered *al-Namārah* stone near Damascus and transferred it to Paris for further examination, had possibly misread the most important part of the inscription—the first line. Based on his reading, it is generally believed today that al-Namārah was the gravestone of king *Umru'ū al-Qays al-Bid'*, the second king of the kingdom of *al-Ḥīrah* and the most significant pre-Islamic Arab leader. Dussaud's reading was partially influenced by an unfortunate mistake in today's Arabic language grammar textbooks. To make matters worse, other scholars who read *al-Namārah* in the past century uncritically strived to uphold Dussaud's reading fundamentals thus reinforcing its equally uncritical acceptance. To prove, at any cost, that *al-Namārah* was *Umru'ū al-Qays* tombstone, some were even willing to present readings that manifestly contradicted the rules of Arabic grammar, geographical facts, and recorded history.

In order to re-read *al-Namārah* inscription, I found it necessary to re-read the *Umm al-Jimāl* Arabic Nabataean inscription as well since the two inscriptions had contained identical words and shared similar historical facts and timeframes. To read the two inscriptions, I had to also read

Raqqush and numerous other Nabataean, Palmyran, and Arabic Musnad inscriptions to study the linguistic usage of similar words and phrases.

Regarding *al-Namārah* inscription, I will, using the tools of the Arabic language, demonstrate through in-depth analytical reading that it is not the tombstone of King *Umru'ū al-Qays bin 'Amrū*, or even about him. Written, most likely, several years after his death, the inscription recorded the important accomplishments of a previously unknown personality, *'Akdī*, who was possibly one of *Umru'ū al-Qays bin 'Amrū* army generals, an Arab tribal leader who collaborated with the Romans, or maybe a top ranking Arab soldier in the Byzantine Roman army. According to my reading, the opening sentence was only a swearing (vow) to the soul of King *Umru' al-Qays bin 'Amrū*, similar to the customary opening sentence used by Arabs and Muslims since the 7th century, *Bism Allāh al-Raḥmān al-Raḥīm* بسم الله الرحمن الرحيم. The main topic of the inscription was the apparent defeat of the prominent *Midhḥij* tribe of southern Arabia in the hands of *'Akdī*'s fighters and the possible subsequent control of Yemen by the Byzantine Roman Empire. The final sentence concluded the inscription by informing the reader about *'Akdī*'s death, maybe in the battlefield, and stating that his parents should be happy and proud of him. This narration is consistent with how soldiers are typically mourned.

I am hopeful that my new readings of *al-Namārah* and *Umm al-Jimāl* inscriptions would prompt scholars in this field to re-examine the current readings in a fundamentally different way. I hope that future history textbooks and the Louvre museum will not state as certain that *al-Namārah* inscription stone was the gravestone or epitaph of King *Umru'ū al-Qays bin 'Amrū*. I also hope that future publications would correct the obvious current readings' errors of the *Umm al-Jimāl* Nabataean inscription. As a linguistic side benefit, I am optimistic that future Arabic language grammar textbooks would cease repeating a common grammatical error regarding simple feminine demonstrative pronouns by re-examining a poem line from *Alfiyyat Ibn Mālik*. Certainly, my new readings could add even more critical, historical, and linguistic importance to *al-Namārah* inscription itself, since the language used in this inscription was clearly and essentially classic Arabic. This can incontrovertibly prove that the grammar and language of the Quran are deeply rooted and developed in Arabia, long before Islam. That is, they are not Islamic or Abbasid inventions as many Western scholars claim.

Because a successful reading of any involved inscription, like *al-Namārah*, requires a comprehensive and organized vision, I divided my reading into convenient sections corresponding to the main topics conceived as preliminary tools to read the full inscription. I have also provided detailed sketches and images to guide the reader into a full visual understanding of the topic of this particular study. Throughout this chapter, I will transliterate (following Library of Congress rules), translate, and write in Arabic various words and phrases to benefit the expert as well as non-expert readers.

3.2 Historical and Geographical Overview

It is problematic to read the inscriptions of *Umm al-Jimāl* and *al-Namārah* without studying first the historical events taking place during the second and third centuries CE — particularly during the early decades of the third century CE and during the reign of King *Umru'ū al-Qays bin 'Amrū* of the city of *al-Hīra*,. The name of this king was mentioned in the first line of *al-Namārah* inscription. Arab and Muslim historians knew *Umru'ū al-Qays bin 'Amrū,* as *Umru'ū al-Qays al-Bid'*, meaning the first. (The desert town of *al-Ḥīrah* is located less than 30 miles south of Babylon, the famed Mesopotamian city that had fallen to the Persians over eight centuries earlier.)

Luckily, *al-Namārah* inscription had provided a precise date that can easily be checked against the more accurate dates provided by the remains left by the three main power players in the Arabian Peninsula during that time: the Persians, the Roman Byzantines, and the Yemenite Arabs. Several other Arab kingdoms existed too, but they were either very weak or tightly under the control of either the Persians or the Romans who fought for the conquest of new territories in the peninsula. After the fall of the northern Arab Nabataean kingdom of Petra at the hands of the Romans (105 CE), the kingdom of Yemen became the only Arab power challenging their rule in the south. Because of repeated Roman attacks, and in order to defend their territory, the Yemeni kings had occasionally forged close ties with the Persians. [6][30]

According to several Muslim scholars, *'Amrū bin 'Uday*, the father of King *Umru'ū al-Qays bin 'Amrū*, was the first king of the ethnically Yemenite Lakhmid kingdom (later, called *al-Manādhirah* Kingdom by the Arabs) to designate *al-Ḥīrah* as the capital city. The *Ḥīrah* Kingdom became the most powerful member of a tribal alliance known as the *Tannūkh* Kingdom, which was established around the 1st century CE by *Mālik bin Māhir* of Yemen. The *Tannūkh* Kingdom controlled a vast area extending from *'Ūmān* in the south to *al-Ḥīrah* and the Syrian Desert near Damascus in the north, occupying the entire west coast of the Persian Gulf, historically known as the Gulf of *Baṣrah*. Islamic Arab era scholars linked the Lakhmid and *Tannūkh* kingdom to the powerful *Ma'ad* tribe of Yemen. The three kings who ruled *Tannūkh* before king *'Amrū bin 'Uday* visited *Ḥīrah* extensively and regularly, but probably had their capital in Bahrain or even Yemen. Most of *Ḥīrah's* original population had eventually moved north to the *Anbār* area before it was made the capital city by King *'Amrū bin 'Uday*. [14][20]

King *'Amrū bin 'Uday's* father was probably a northern Arab. His mother was the sister of *Judhaymah al-Abrash* who was the first king and the founder of the *Tannūkh* Kingdom dynasty. He maintained close relations with the Persians and ruled before and after the time of King *Ardashīr bin Bābik*

(224-241 CE), the first king of the third and last Sassanid dynasty, and the son of the Zaradust priest, *Bābik*, who had earlier toppled the last king of the second Sassanid dynasty.[15]

It seems that *Judhaymah al-Abrash*, a Yemenite Arab, had decided to offer his sister to a northern Arab from the *Ḥīrah* area to establish closer blood relation with the northern tribes. The practice of marrying sisters and daughters to link with other tribes is quite common among Arab tribes. As we shall see later, both of the words *Tannūkh* and *Judhaymah* will appear briefly in the important Arabic Nabataean inscription, *Umm al-Jimāl,* found south of Damascus and believed to be dated 250 CE. According to sources, King *'Amrū bin 'Uday* took advantage of the temporary weakening of the Sassanid Persian Empire after the death of King *Ardashīr bin Bābik* and decided to invade the Persian-controlled Arab areas of Bilād al-'Irāq (Mesopotamia) with the help of the Romans and the Arab tribes north and west of *Ḥīrah.*[20][30] His action had therefore reversed the traditional alliance of the previous, purely Yemenite, kings of *Tannūkh* with the Persians.

After the death of King *'Amrū bin 'Uday* in the year 288 CE, his son, *Umru'ū al-Qays bin 'Amrū* took over and decided to expand on his father's attacks even further to include all Persian-controlled areas in Arabia. He was the first Arab leader who seriously attempted to unify all parts of the Arabian Peninsula in a single kingdom challenging both the Romans and Persians, and was therefore considered the most revered man in Arabia before Islam. Taking advantage of further conflicts within the Sassanid Persian royal family, he had even crossed the Persian (Arabic) Gulf to raid the heartland of Persia. Pre-Islamic Arabic poetry spoke of several virulent raids by the Arab tribes against the Persians in Bilād al-'Irāq. It is known that poems are the most important record-keeping evidence of the Arab tribes who traditionally relied on memory, not writing, to document their events. King *Umru'ū al-Qays* succeeded in bringing most of the Arabian Peninsula under his control except for the powerful Yemen and the Roman-controlled Arab kingdom in Syria, known as *al-Ghasāsinah* Kingdom. History recorded that, because the Roman supported the campaigns of Umru'ū al-Qays, the Persians were forced to accept a deal with the Romans (298 CE) whereby they ceded many of their previously captured territories in Mesopotamia.

A decade later, a new powerful king took over Sassanid Persia. He was *Shabur II* (309-379 CE) known to the Arabs under the nickname *Dhū al-Aktāf* ذو الاكتاف (the owner of the shoulders.) It was believed that he had pierced his Arab prisoners' shoulders to tie them together after captivity. *Shabur II* regained control over most of the areas lost to the Romans and their Arab allies. It was said that he had captured *Ḥīrah*, the seat of King *Umru'ū al-Qays*, after a bloody battle in the year 225 CE, three years before the date mentioned in *al-Namārah* inscription.[14][15] However, it is not known whether King *Umru'ū al-Qays* had survived that battle. Only after the discovery of *al-Namārah* and subsequent Dussaud's reading had experts claimed that King *Umru'ū al-Qays* had escaped to

Damascus and died in the city of Bosra on December 7th, 223 Bosra (equivalent to 228 CE), which is the date mentioned in the inscription.

I have to mention, however, that there is no other evidence supporting the above claim except the supposed evidence of *al-Namārah* inscription. Nonetheless, based on my reading of the first line of the inscription as a vow to his soul, I am prone to think that he died earlier, possibly in the battle of *Ḥīrah*, 325 CE. After the death of king *Umru'ū al-Qays*, the Roman and Persians fought extensively all over Arabia until the year 363 CE when they finally signed a treaty acknowledging Persian supremacy over Iraq. [15]

Consequent to fierce Arab attacks on the Sassanid forces stationed in Mesopotamia (330 -370 CE), descendants of king *Umru'ū al-Qays* were allowed to go back to *al-Ḥīrah* and rule under the protection of the Persians. Finally, the Muslim Arabs defeated the Persians in the battle of al-*Qādisiyyah* (638 CE) which effectively put an end to the Sassanid Empire. [14][30]

In the early decades of the 4th century CE, Yemen, the seat of the oldest known Arab kingdoms in the peninsula, was a prime target for both the Romans and the Persians. The Yemenites were generally referred to by the rest of the Arabs as *al-Ḥimīriyyīn*, and depending on whom and when, Yemen was additionally known as *Midhḥij* or *Ma'ad*. The tribes of *Midhḥij* and *Ma'ad* are the largest and most powerful tribes in Yemen. Being the most powerful among the Arab kingdoms of that time, Yemen had maintained its status as an independent kingdom.

As mentioned earlier, King *Umru'ū al-Qays* was never able to control Yemen. In fact, during his time around the year 300 CE, a Yemenite king named *Shammar Yuhar'ish*, was able to unify Yemen including *Haḍramawt* to create a powerful kingdom. [6] If logic matters, It would be impossible that a defeated king *Umru'ū al-Qays,* who had just lost his capital city of *al-Ḥīrah* in a bloody battle around the year 225 CE, would accomplish the highest military victory of his times— the conquest of Yemen— at the same time of *al-Namārah* (328 CE.)

Reportedly, king *Shammar Yuhar'ish* had maintained close relations with the Persians by sending a diplomatic mission to the Sasanian court at Ctesiphon, *al-Madā'in*, Iraq. [6] *Khawārizmī*, a prominent Muslim scholar who lived during the early Islamic centuries called him *Shimr Yar'ish* or *Abū Karab Bin Ifrīqis,* which could mean he was of African origins as per the use of the word *Ifrīqis.* No diacritic vowel was placed on the first word *shimr* شمر. This could indicate that his name was either *Shimr* — a classic Arabic name—, or *Shammar* — a well-known name of a prominent Arab tribe in Northern *Najd.* I do believe though, it is the former because *al-Namārah* inscription has one *mīm* letter in the name. *Khawārizmī* further wrote that King *Shimr* was called *Yar'ish* (trembling) because he was suffering of a nervous condition that made him tremble. According to *Khawārizmī*, King *Shimr*

Yar'ish was, as claimed by some, nicknamed king *Dhū al-Qirnayn* (the one with two horns) contrary to the belief of many who thought this was a nickname for the Macedonian conqueror, Alexander the Great. Further, *Khawārizmī* listed King *Shimr Yar'ish* as the 20th king of Yemen before Islam and listed king *Umru'ū al-Qays bin 'Amrū* as the 21st king of *al-Ḥīrah* before Islam. [14] This means, the two kings had ruled approximately during the same period. In fact, the dates reported by *Khawārizmī's* coincide well with the dates provided by historians today. Most importantly, this coincidence would make it highly probable that King *Shimr Yar'ish* was indeed the king of Yemen during the times of *al-Namārah* inscription.

While it is not impossible that King *Umru'ū al-Qays bin 'Amrū* could have died in the year 328 CE, the historical evidence, including *al-Namārah* inscription, indicates otherwise. Again, I do believe that he died between the years 309 CE after *Shabur* II took power, in 325 CE, the year *al-Ḥīrah* was captured. As we shall see later, when reading *al-Namārah*, the historical analysis above could become vital to the understanding of the events, dates, and names appearing in the inscription.

3.3 Rereading the *Umm al-Jimāl* Nabataean Arabic Inscription

As mentioned earlier, according to Western scholars, among the numerous Nabataean inscriptions discovered so far, only three were written fully in the Arabic language. Dated 328 CE, *al-Namārah* was the latest inscription of the three. The two earlier inscriptions are *Umm al-Jimāl,* found in the same area, around Damascus, where *al-Namārah* was found, and *Raqqūsh*, found in *Madā'in Ṣālaḥ*, not very far south of Damascus in Northern *Ḥijāz*. Both areas were previously Nabataean territories. *Raqqūsh* indicated the date of 267 CE while *Umm al-Jimāl*, which explicitly mentioned the names *Judhaymah* and *Tannūkh,* was dated around the year 260 CE, clearly a successful estimate when checked against our geographical and historical review in the previous section. The two inscriptions are therefore older than *al-Namārah* by at least 60 or even 70 years. This would make them useful references for this study. As we shall see later, reading the three inscriptions together is valuable for the separate reading of each one of them correctly.

While *Raqqūsh* and *Umm al-Jimāl* were decidedly gravestones, *al-Namārah* could be either a gravestone or an honoring monument (I shall come back to this later.) Further, as *Raqqūsh* and *Namārah* included several text lines, *Umm al-Jimāl* was brief. Unlike in *Namārah Umm al-Jimāl* the language used in *Raqqūsh* was not classic Arabic entirely.

Moreover, the Nabataean script used in both inscriptions was not solidly cursive, and did not follow closely current Arabic cursive rules. Both inscriptions clearly started with the word *dnh* دنه, but scholars read the word differently in

Raqqūsh where the first letter *dāl* was slightly attached to the second letter *nūn* forming another possible shape. The Arabic word *qabrū* (tomb) was mentioned three times in *Raqqūsh*, and was read as such by all scholars. The same exact word though in *Umm al-Jimāl* was read as a person's name, *Fahrū*, which clearly was an error, as I will demonstrate later. [11]

Current *Raqqūsh* Nabataen tracing	letter-for-letter Arabic transcription
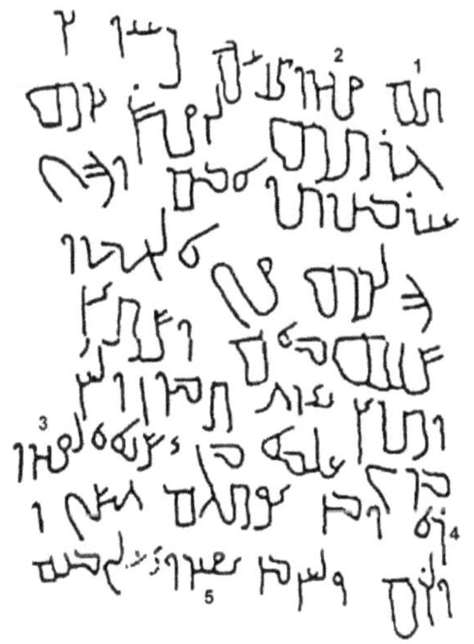	دنه قبرو صنعه كعبو بر حذتت لرقوش برت عبذ منرتو امه وهي هلكت في الحجرو سنت مئه وستين وتنين بيرخ تموز ولعن مري علما من يشنا القبرو ذا ومن يفتحه خشي و ولذه ولعن من يقبر ويعلي منه

Figure (3.1) Arabic Nabataean inscription *Raqqūsh,* dated 267 CE, with author's improved tracing. Numbers added to facilitate discussion.

Unfortunately, I was unable to view enough photographic details of either inscription. However, for the purpose of this study, I feel it is adequate to rely on the available Nabataean

Photographs of the *Umm al-Jimāl* inscription stone

Author's Nabataean tracing	Current Nabataean tracing

Author's letter-for-letter Arabic transcription	Current letter-for-letter Arabic transcription
دنه نفسو قبر فرء بر سلي ربو جذيمت مملك تنوخ	دنه نفسو فهرو بر سلي ربو جذيمت ملك دنوخ

Figure (3.2) Arabic Nabataean inscription of *Umm al-Jimāl*, dated around 250 CE, with current and author's tracing and reading for comparison. Numbers added to facilitate discussion.

tracing of *Raqqūsh.* A word of caution: without retracing it personally, I would be reluctant to offer a full letter-by-letter transcription or modern Arabic reading.

As for *Umm al-Jimāl*, examining a high-resolution picture of the stone was very sufficient to illustrate the validity of my new tracings of a few key words in the inscription. Accordingly, I provided here the above original photo and another zoomed-in photoshoped image of the eroded re-traced area of the stone, along with current tracing — a letter-by-letter Arabic transcription and corresponding modern Arabic translation. Based on this new tracing, a new detailed reading emerges that significantly differs from the current reading.

In Figure 3.1, the first word in *Raqqūsh* and *Umm al-Jimāl* was clearly a three letter word *dnh*, but scholars differed both on its tracing and reading in *Raqqūsh*. Some read it as *th* ته, claiming it was an Arabic simple feminine demonstrative pronoun; this is neither correct nor possible since the following word *qabr* is a masculine noun. [23] Others read it as the Arabic letter *dhāl*, probably for the simple masculine demonstrative *dhā* ذا, which would contradict directly with the reading of word #4 in the same inscription showing *dhā* spelled as letter *dāl* with dot above followed by *alif.* [11] Yet, few traced it as *dh.n.h* for *dhnah* ذنه claiming this was a northern Arabic feminine demonstrative pronoun.

However, most scholars traced word #1 in both inscriptions as *dnh,* a word present in numerous other fully Nabataean inscriptions, and read it as an assumingly Aramaic masculine demonstrative. I traced it in both as *dnh,* too, but I read it as *adnāh*, أدناه, a word used in Arabic to point to a nearby object or text that is located generally below the horizontal visual level. The beginning *alif* with *hamzah* above was possibly omitted because the word was possibly pronounced *dnāh* دناه, in the local Arab Nabataean dialect. *Raqqūsh* and most other inscriptions used several local dialect words, notably *bir* for *bin*, or *'abdh* for *'abd.* Otherwise, beginning *alif-hamzah* could have been omitted, just as the second *alif* between the letters *nūn* and *hā'* was omitted, consistent with Arabic writing throughout the 8th century CE, as evident in all available inscriptions and manuscripts.

The Arabic word *adnāh* is utilized extensively today in the meaning of "see by, or near, you", "see below" or "the following below." It can be used effectively as a gender neutral demonstrative in the meaning of *hunā* هنا as in "here" or "here in". When I searched for the use of this word in older Arabic references, I was surprised that I could not find any documented evidence of its usage in that contest. Assuming my reading is correct, which it is, this would make the two inscriptions the earliest Arabic references documenting the usage of the word in such manner. The word *danā*, a classic Arabic verb, means "became physically close or near to someone or some object." [13] Among numerous examples, the Quran (53:9) used it in ثُمَّ دَنَا فَتَدَلَّى فَكَانَ قَابَ قَوْسَيْنِ أَوْ أَدْنَى. Also, the Islamic *Ḥadīth* used *'adnāh min nafsih* to describe how

Prophet Muhammad had a visiting Arab king sitting — physically — very close to him. [17][26] Less likely, this word could be *idnah* إدنه for the imperative: "come close to,"omitting beginning *alif-hamzah* with *kasrah*. Regardless of how one would read the first word *dnh*, the most important fact is that it was explicitly used as a word pointing to a masculine object: *qabr* قبر and consistently used as an opening word for most Nabataean gravestones, including these two.

In *Umm al-Jimāl* scholars spelled the next word after *dnh,* as *n.f.sh.ū,* and read it نفشو supposedly from a "Semitic" feminine noun *napš'* or from Arabic *nafs* as in the Quran (89:27) يَا أَيَّتُهَا النَّفْسُ الْمُطْمَئِنَّةُ. This same word can also be pronounced in Arabic as *nafas* in the sense of "inhalation or breathing" which would be a masculine noun. It is not clear, how scholars pronounced this word found in various Nabataean inscriptions as *napš* or *napiš,* still, in both cases it would be a feminine noun. Even before analyzing the meaning and usage of *nafsh*, one can already suspect through *Umm al-Jimāl* that its current reading is questionable since the word *dnh* was used in *Raqqūsh*, and many other Nabataean inscriptions to point to *qabrū*, a masculine noun. This contradiction can only be solved by relating *dnh* as *adnāh,* a neutral Arabic demonstrative pronoun, as I have argued above. As we shall see later, *dnh* was used to point to a feminine noun, *mqbrt',* in at least one Nabataean inscription from Petra. Alternatively, *dnh* could be pointing to a third masculine noun and the second word *nafsū* is not a noun (I shall discuss this soon.) Still, it is also possible that the word *nafsū* was actually *naqshū* نقشُ, for the classic Arabic masculine noun, *naqsh* (etching), used to indicate the act of writing or sketching on all mediums including epitaph's stones and even sand. [13][22] Unlike the Nabataean letter *fā', which* is a left starting loop with a right side downward vertical stem, the letter *qāf* is a circle attached in the middle to a downward vertical stem. This was evident in the three inscriptions.

Reading the second word (let us call it #2) of *Umm al-Jimāl* as *naqshū* can conflict with the current reading of word #3 of the inscription, which is thought to be *Fihrū* for *Fihr* فهر, a classic Arabic name. Even though it is possible to read the opening phrase (based on our reading of the second word as *naqshu*) as *adnāh naqshu Fihrū bin Sāllī*, after examining the photo of Figure 4.1 and even according to the current tracing it is clear that word #3 of *Umm al-Jimāl* is not *Fihrū.* It is *qabrū*, followed by a first name containing the letters *fā' , rā'* and *alif/hamzah* as in *Fara'* فَرء or Firā' فِراء, an old Arabic male name meaning "wild donkey" which is known for its excellent skills to escape hunters! This name was possibly modified to *Faru'* فرُء according to old Northern Arabic and Aramaic practice of using *wāw* sound at the end of names.

In the Hadith, Prophet Muhammad told *Abū Sufyān:* "You are as they say, all hunting is in the belly of the wild donkey'". Translated from the Arabic text: يا أبا سفيان! أنت كما قال القائل : كل الصيد في جوف الفرا . [13] The three partially damaged letters for *Faru'* can clearly be traced in the subsequent space, which is suspiciously wide for an intentional space! To illustrate my point, I provided a partial image of the stone utilizing the Brush Strokes filter utility in Photoshop to emphasize stroke edges and reveal the new traced letters. The third word (we indicated with #3) has only one prominent long horizontal stroke connected to the letter *rā'* on the left, just as it was the case with medial letter *bā'* in *qabru* of *Raqqūsh* (words #3, #4, and #5). There is a short downward line pointing to the left that seems to be stone discoloration, not a stroke. Nevertheless, even if it were a stroke, the formed shape would surely not resemble the Nabataean letter *hā'*. A second short, left-pointing, downward line just below the letter *rā'* is not a stroke either, as it resembles an extensive crack. The only difference between the word *qabr* we see in *Umm al-Jimāl* and the one in *Raqqūsh* is that the upward line stroke forming the medial letter *bā'* in *Umm al-Jimāl* was not vertical. Instead, it was pointing left as it was the case with the previous word *nafsū* and the following word *Fara'*— clearly a scribe hand-writting style. One can even spot another faded parallel, left-tilted line connecting to the horizontal stroke of that letter thus forming a classic Nabataean medial letter *bā'*, slightly affected by a possible scriber style or error, stone discoloration and crack, or a subsequent alteration. Moreover, the first letter of this word is clearly *qāf*, not *fā'*, which can easily be compared to the many letters *qāf* in *al-Namārah* and *Raqqūsh*.

Reading word #3 in *Umm al-Jimāl* as *qabrū* or *qabr* would allow more possibilities for the meaning and usage of the previous word. An alternative to my reading of the word as *naqshū*, could be *nafsū,* but in the meaning of *nafsuhū*, *hūwa nafsuhū*, for "itself", referring to *qabr*. This reading would fit well with reading *dnh,* either as a masculine, or as a neutral demonstrative. The beginning phrase could then be "this itself is the tomb of" similar to *hadhā hūwa qabr* هذا هو قبر, a standard usage on gravestones in Arabic, or *hadhā nafsuhū qabr* هذا نفسُهُ قبر. To summarize, an initial modern Arabic reading of the opening phrase of *Umm al-Jimāl* inscription could be either *dnh naqshū qabr Faru' bir Sāllī* هذا نقشُ قبر فرُء بن سالّي, or *dnh nafshū qabr Faru' bir Sāllī* هذا هو قبر فرُء بن سالّي.

However, I should now bring attention to a curious fact: my reading of the opening phrase in *Umm al-Jimāl* as *nafsū qabrū* or *nafsū qabr* is intriguingly identical to the usual opening phrase in the Arabic *Musnad* script found on eastern Arabian tombs' inscriptions: *nafs.w.qabr* نفس و قبر. King *Judhaymah*, whose name appears in the *Umm al-Jimāl* inscription, was linked to the eastern Arabian area where the *Tannūkh* kingdom was supposedly situated before moving to *al-Ḥīrah*, as I indicated in my review section above. Most scholars read that phrase as *nafs wa-qabr* and translated it as "funerary monument and grave of", by assuming that the middle *wāw* was "and". Based on this and other readings of Nabataean, Hebrew, and Palmyra inscriptions, most scholars assumed that the word *n.p.š* (also *n.f.š* or *nafs*) was used individually in the sense of "funerary monument" or "memorial stele" (we shall discuss that in detail later.) Analyzing the *Musnad* script is outside the scope of this chapter, however, the very likely meaning of this phase should be روح و قبر "soul and grave of." Alternatively, with the striking similarity between the *Musnad* letters *fā'* and *'ayn,* both in the *Musnad Liḥyanī* and *Saba'ī* styles, the word *nafs* could also be *na'sh* نعش which is the classic Arabic word for coffin or deathbed. It is highly unlikely that the word *nafs* was commonly used among the Arabs in the meaning of "memorial stele," but would suddenly disappear from usage, without a trace, only a couple of centuries later! Most important, even if the word was indeed *nafs* (not *nafsū*) in these few Musnad inscriptions, it is extremely crucial to observe that it was consistently used together with *qabr* as an opening phrase or prologue. None of the available burial Musnad inscriptions used the word *nafs* alone as a main introductory phrase preceding a name.[5][31] As mentioned earlier, based on the *Umm al-Jimāl* evidence, the phrase *nafs.w.qabr* could have been used to mean *hadhā huwa qabr* هذا هو قبر "this is the grave of," consistent with all other Arabic usage throughout history.

In Arabic, the three letters word *nafs* is rather complex; consequently, I have some explaning to do. The root of the word is *nafas,* meaning "breath" from which two main types of usage were derived. The first includes "soul", "life", "person", or "being"; the second "self" as in "same", "identical", "itself", "himself", and "herself". [13] This first primary usage could even be traced to the Babylonian Epic of Gilgamesh where the god-man name *Ut.napištu.m* (the Sumerian mythological prototype which inspired the story of Biblical Noah who survived the flood) can literally be translated as "eternal great soul-being". Just like Arabic, Hebrew used *napšā* and Aramaic Syriac used *napištu.* The Nabataean tomb inscriptions used *l.napš.h* extensively in the meaning of "for himself"; but the words *napšā* and *napštā* had also appeared in few other cases. [11] Palmyrenes used to portray the dead either in relief or in statues placed on tombs. [24] They usually referred to a statue as *ṣalam* (as in Arabic *ṣanam*). But they might have had also referred to it — although rarely — as *napšā*, or *napeš* to mean "the same" or "the identical", which 1) it conforms to the second main usage of the word in Arabic just mentioned, and 2) it fits well when naming a personal statue. The Nabataeans, instead, used an architectonic form (a cone topped by inflorescence) placed on a cylindrical or square base that they might have, arguably, referred to as *napšā,* or *napeš*, too. These memorial stones can be carved or engraved into rock faces with an identifying inscription that occasionally accompany them and is normally located in the base. [24] [29]

Although unlikely, it is possible that the Nabataeans had explicitly used the word *nafash* for their architectonic-shaped personal memorial monuments, instead of their frequently used word *naṣb* (as in Arabic نصب,) and for monuments they erected for their idols. It is my firm opinion that scholars who read *Umm al-Jimāl*, which was discovered after *al-Namārah*, rushed to replicate, verbatim, Dussaud and other scholars' readings of the word *napš* to mean"memorial Monument" or "funerary Monument". Some even stretched its meaning to *shahidat qabr*, which can be translated to "tombstone" or "burial monument". To emphasize the usage of the word *napš*, Healey referenced *Le Nabatéen, by* Gantineau who defined the word as such, offering only two Nabataean inscriptions as evidence: *Umm al-Jimāl* which Gantineau called the *Fahrū* inscription, and *al-Namārah*!

In his indispensable book about *Madā'in Ṣāliḥ* tombs inscriptions, Healey further opined that this "Pyramidal stele carved in the rock" could explain the "mysterious" absence of inscriptions from the numerous tombs found in the city of Petra, which he believes had banned tombs inscriptions. [10] Surprisingly though, the *Umm al-Jimāl* stone and its inscription do not even conform to the physical and inscriptional characteristics of a typical so-called Nabataean *napš*, which rarely included any type of inscription except for an occasional name. Furthermore, the majority of the hundreds of Nabataean tombs' inscriptions found so far had consistently used the introductory phrase *dnh kapr'* or *dnh qabr'*. My reading of the two inscriptions listed by Healey, in which he read the word *napš'* in the meaning of "burial monument" and the other word, *napšt'*, as "two burial monuments," [10] led me to a different conclusion.

My initial analysis of the two inscriptions, the Madeba and Strasbourg inscriptions revealed that the word *napš* was actually used in its usual Arabic language meanings of "identical", "same", "similar", or "itself". The opening phrase of Strasbourg inscription as of his tracing *dʾ napšʾ dy ʾabr br mqymw dy bnh lh* was possibly ذا هو نفس الذي لأبار بن مقيمو الذي بناه له, or "This is the same [tomb] that belong to *ʾabār* son of *mqymw* which his father built for him". The word *dy* is similar to the Arabic word usage of *dhī* and *dhū* in the meaning of "which belongs to". [13] Also notice that *dʾ* (or *dā*), which is spelled exactly as the classic Arabic masculine demonstrative *dhā*, is unlikely a Nabataean feminine demonstrative as believed by some scholars today. Clearly, it was used in the Nabataeean *Raqqūsh* inscription (the fourth word we indicated as #4) after a masculine noun, *qabrū*, not a feminine! In fact, *dʾ* was not used in this and several other Nabatatean inscriptions listed by Healey as a simple demonstrative pronoun, but as a neutral gender identity or emphasis pronoun. Very likely, its usage is related to that of classic Arabic as in: *dhā*, *huwa dhā* or *dhā huwa* as in *dhātih* (ذاته) ذا هو، هو ذا for masculine, and in *hiya dhā* or *dhā hiyah* as in *dhātihā* (ذاتها) ذا هي، هي ذا for feminine.

As for Madeba inscription, the opening phrase *dnh mqbrtʾ wtrty napštʾ dy ʿlʾ mnh dy ʿbd* was likely ادناه (هذه) هي المقبرة والثلاثة المشابهة لها التي اعلى منها التي, or "This is the tomb, and the three identical ones that are above it, which ..."

Or saying it in other words "Below is the tomb, and the other three that look just like it that sit above it that ..." The letter *tā'* in *napšt'* is likely referring to feminine noun *mqbrt'*. The number word was possibly *tlty*, from the Nabataean word for "three" *tlt*, not *trty*, which Healey linked to *tryn,* supposedly a Nabataean number word meaning "two." Supporting this argument, the inscription listed three, not two, owners after the opening phrase. I do believe though that the number word *tryn,* for two, is actually *tnyn,* because all other Nabataean number words are identical to Arabic and the Nabataean letters *nūn* and *ra'* can easily be mixed up. This can be verified in *Raqqūsh*, where the first word of the sixth line is clearly *wtnyn,* not *wtryn.* Still, even if the number was actually "two," the Madeba opening sentence would be ادناه (هذه) هي المقبرة والاثنين المشابهة لها (عينُها) التي اعلى منها التي.. or "Here below is (or this is) the tomb and the two identical to it (that sit) above it, which..."

As a conclussion, I am convinced that the best way to analyze the language used in any Nabataean inscription is to rely on classic Arabic first. I see no solid evidence to presume that the word *nafsh* or *nafs,* in an opening phrase of an Arabic or Nabataean burial inscription, would necessarily mean "funerary monument" or "memorial monument". Furthermore, it is vital to observe that the word *qabr* was consistently used whenever a burial place was involved, whether in *Musnad*, Nabataean, or Palmyrene inscriptions. It is not impossible that the phrase *nasfu qabr* could have been used to mean *shāhidat qabr* or "grave marker" (stele), which may lead us to believe that the word *nafs* alone could have been used to mean "marker" or *shāhidah.* However, in such case, it is of paramount importance to observe that there is no solid evidence in any *Musnad* or Nabataen inscription where the word *nafs* alone was used to mean stele, let alone memorial monument. It is very unlikely, therefore, that the *'Umm al-Jimāl* inscription was part of a monument that was erected without an actual grave in a cemetery, which in turn, is the only possible case that can justify using the word *nafs*, by itself, in the meaning of "memorial monument" in an opening phrase.

Before analyzing the final line of the *Umm al-Jimāl* inscription, it is worth mentioning that although this inscription was not a bilingual inscription, it was discovered next to a separate stone with a Greek inscription, which appears to be an exact translation of the Nabataean text (see Figure 3.2.) Despite my belief that the Nabataean inscription should be the main reference to use in our ongoing analysis (pronouncing Arabic names can be deceiving in the Greek translation), I will analyze the first four or five words of the Greek inscription which, by all accounts, seems to support our new reading of the Nabataean text. Although there were no spaces in the Greek inscription, as evident in Figure 3.2, the first five words seem are Η СΤΗΛΗ ΑΥΤΗ ΦΕΡΟΥ СΟΛΛΕΟΥ. According to my reading of the Greek text, the first line can be translated in English as "This is the stele (grave marker) of Feroo Salleoo".

Clearly, the first name was ΦΕΡΟΥ or Feroo, not Fehroo — there is no indication of the guttural sound of the Arabic letter *hā'* anywhere in the word, unless the reader was invoking past Phoenician letter *he* origin of the Greek E! My belief, the inscription used the Greek sound OY (sounds like oo as in wood) at the end of the first name ΦΕΡΟΥ to substitute for either *Alif-Hamzah* or *Dhammah-Hamzah*. You may recall, according to my reading of the Nabataean inscription, the word was either *Fara'* or *Faru'*. The sound OY was repeated at the end of the last name COΛΛΕΟΥ (Salleoo) too — in spite of the existence of the letter *Yā'* at the end of that word in the Nabataean text. The repeated use of the sound OY further indicates that the first name was not necessarily ending with a *wāw* as experts (evidently depending mainly on the Greek text) mistakenly assumed. I will discuss again this Aramaic and Northern Arabic usage of the sound *wāw* after names, later. In addition, using the word CTHΛH (Stele) would not necessarily mean that this word was an exact translation of *nafs,* because translating a text is not linear; that is, it is not a

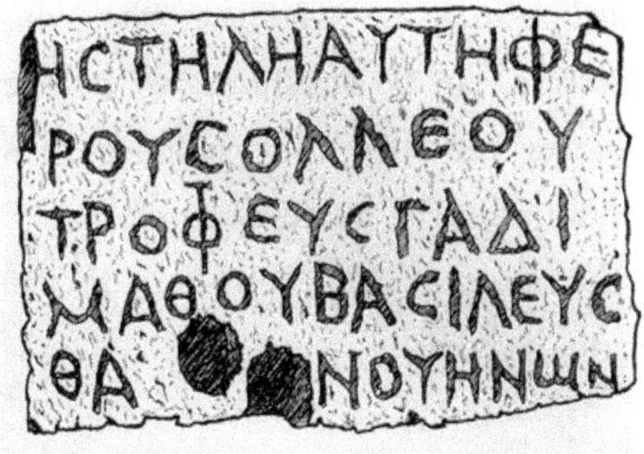

Figure (3.3) Transcription of the he Greek *Umm al-Jimāl* inscription.

word-for-word process. At best, this type of usage could mean that some Nabataean Arabs used *nafsu qabr* combined to mean stele.

More observations on the *Umm al-Jimāl* inscription reading include the following:

1. Word #4 was read *malk* for Arabic king. However, after careful tracing of the Nabataean text, we can clearly see a second letter *mim*; therefore, the correct reading should be *mmlk*, for classic Arabic *mumallik* مُمَلِّك, which literally means, "the one who crowned or gave kingship to"; meaning in current context: "the founder of the dynasty of". Moreover, reading word #4 in this way would accurately fit the meaning conveyed by word #5 *Tannūkh,* king *Judhaymah's* tribe*,* which, as you will see below, was inaccurately read as *Dannūkh.*
2. Word #5 (*Tannūkh*): The first letter of this word is clearly a Nabataean letter *tā',* not a *dāl.* As stated earlier in our history review section*,* King *Judhaymah al-Abrash*, *Umru'ū al-Qays'* uncle, was the founder of the *Tannūkh* kingdom, or, using the inscription words, he was the one who crowned them. This assertion can be substantiated by the fact that Arab history never recorded the existence of a tribe or kingdom in Arabia under the name *Dannukh.*
3. The final phrase would then be *mumallik Tannūkh*, or "the one who started the Tannukh dynasty".

To summarize, a leter-by-letter transcription of *Umm al-Jimāl* is as follows: "*dnh nfsu qbr fra bir sali rabu jdhimat mmlik tannukh.*" Line-by-line, the Arabic text is: دنه نفسو قبر فرء - بر سلي ربو جذيمت - مملك تنوخ. In modern Arabic it says: أدناه (هذا) هو قبر فرءُ بن سالّي مُربّي جُذيمة مؤسس مملكة تَنّوخ, or أدناه روح وقبر فرءُ بن سالّي مُربّي جُذيمة مؤسس مملكة تَنّوخ. Translated to English, it says: "Below is (itself) the tomb of *Faru' bin Sālī*, custodian of *Judhaymah,* crowner of *Tannūkh,*" or "This is the soul and tomb of *Faru' bin Sālī,* custodian of *Judhaymah,* crowner of *Tannūkh."*

Before proceeding to the next section, I need to elaborate on the important usage of the letter *wāw* at the end of nouns. For example, notice the words *qabrū* for *qabr*, *Ka'bū* for *Ka'b*, and *Ḥijrū*, for *Ḥijr* in *Raqqūsh*. This practice is consistent with that of most pre-Islamic northern Arabic inscriptions that are available today, whether written in Nabataean or Arabic *Jazm* scripts. As we shall see later, *al-Namārah* added *wāw* after all names too. The Arabic inscriptions of al-*Jazzāz* (410 AD), *Sakkākah* (late 4th Century), *Zabad* (512 AD), and *Ḥarrān* (568 AD) had all added *wāw* after the names. This is a known Aramaic and Northern Arabic usage which was likely incorporated into theses languages due to Greek or Roman influence. [1][21] In fact, the use of *wāw* is by itself a solid proof that most, if not all, Arab tribes which migrated north — centuries before the *Tannūkh* kingdom era, especially the ancestors of the Nabataeans — had heavily adapted the neighboring Aramaic culture. On the other hand, classic Arabic teaches us that the *wāw* of *ʿAmrū* is added to distinguish the Arabic name *ʿAmr* from *ʿUmar*. My belief is that *wāw* originally existed in the name *ʿAmrū*, and should be pronounced, at least when it is applied to *ʿAmrū bin ʿUday*, father of *Umruʾū al-Qays*, who was likely a northern Arab, not a Yemenite.

3.4 Arabic Grammar Prelude: Is *tī* a Simple Feminine Demonstrative Pronoun?

Before reading *al-Namārah*, it is important to thoroughly examine the first word of the inscription. The word is clear and legible and has two letters: *tī* تي. Dussaud claimed this word was an Arabic simple feminine demonstrative pronoun, meaning "this is." Throughout the 20th century, all subsequent readers of *al-Namārah* agreed with him without any debate!

For example, in his comprehensive reading of 1985, Bellamy allocated only one line to address the word where he referred his readers to consult with two old reference books for further explanation.[7] The first book was an enhanced English translation of an older Arabic grammar textbook that was initially published in 1857 in German; and the second was a British book published in 1930 and had for a subject the history of the Arabs of the western peninsula.

The author of the first book listed among his other references, *Alfiyyat Ibn Mālik*, a long Arabic poem comprising one thousand verses summarizing the grammar of the Arab language. [32] Written by the great Arabic linguist, *'Ibn Mālik*, about eight centuries ago, the *Alfiyyah* is the most authoritative reference for textbooks on modern Arabic grammar. Notably absent from his references was an important Arabic language reference book, *Lisān al-'Arab*, written during the same period of *Alfiyyah* by another great Arabic linguist, *Ibn Manẓūr*. Both of these references are manuscripts that became widely available after the emergence of Arabic typography in the 18th century.

Being a collection of poems, *Alfiyyat Ibn Mālik* is only useful when read by a professional linguist. In fact, many revered scholars, like *Ibn 'Aqīl*, wrote volumes of manuscripts to explain it. Unfortunately, these scholars had to rely on a manuscript that could have possibly included unclear words, missing verses, and scribes' mistakes. Contemporary scholars mainly rely on these older explanations of the manuscript, known as *tafsīr*. On the other hand, *Lisān al-'Arab*, predating *Alfiyyat Ibn Mālik,* was written with explicit explanations by the original author along with generous examples from pre-Islamic poetry and the Quran.

To summarize the simple demonstrative pronouns in Arabic grammar, *Ibn Mālik* wrote a single line (verse) of a poem:

بِذا لِمُفْرَدٍ مُذكـَّرٍ أَشـِرْ   بِذي وذِهْ ؟؟ تا على الأنثى اقتَصِرْ

Translated into English the line says "use *dhā* to point to a masculine noun, and limit yourself to *dhī* and *dhih ?? tā* for a feminine." In the original manuscript, the unclear and disputed word between *dhih* and *tā* (marked with two question marks by the author) was either a genuine word, a corrected word, or a crossed out word. Researching several old *tafsīr* books, I discovered that scholars had read this unclear word quite differently. [8] However, most scholars of the Islamic Arab civilization era decided to omit this unclear word and simply list the only three known Arabic simple demonstrative pronouns for a feminine noun: *dhī*, *dhih*, and *tā*. I am listing below in Arabic a few of these verse readings.

بذا لِمفْرَدٍ مُذكّرٍ أشرْ   بذي وذِهْ تا على الأنثى اقتَصِرْ
بِذا لِمُفْرَدٍ مُذكّرٍ أَشِرْ   بِذي وذِهْ تي تا على الأنثى اقتَصِرْ
بذا لِمفْرَدٍ مُذكّرٍ أشرْ   بذي وذِهْ نسى نا على الأنثى اقتَصِرْ
بذا لِمفْرَدٍ مُذكّرٍ أشرْ   بذي وذِهْ تي ته على الأنثى اقتَصِرْ

Apparently, some overzealous and persistent scholars decided to read this unfortunate scribe's error by replacing it with one or more words. Almost all of these scholars justified their readings in Islamic religious terms. Those who claimed it was *tī*, explained how this reading would be consistent with the Islamic teachings allowing four wives for one man [sic]! With the passing of time, more Islamic scholars joined in. Some had even claimed that Arabic has nine simple demonstrative pronouns for a feminine noun. Some even claimed that, unlike a man, a woman does not have a specific social status; therefore, she must be pointed to with multiple pronouns. To conclude, unfortunately, the Arabic grammar textbook listed by Bellamy, which most likely was Dussaud's main reference too, listed nine simple demonstrative pronouns including *tī*, as many Arabic grammar textbooks do today.

It is inconclusive whether the scribe's error in the manuscript of *Alifiyyat Ibn Mālik* was the reason behind these claims. Clearly, *Ibn Mālik* used the word, *Iqtaṣir*, which is an imperative verb meaning "limit yourself to." My impression is that some Muslim scholars during *Ibn Mālik's* time were busy making up feminine pronouns to support their religious claims and theories, a trend that evidently prompted *Ibn Mālik* to write his grammatical poem in that strong manner to correct them. [12] A simple online search today would lead to more of such Muslim scholars who are overly obsessed with the topic of females and Islam. Ironically — I must observe — to support their arguments, some Muslim scholars desperately tried to explain that the imperative verb *iqtaṣir* was referring to the masculine in the meaning of "do not use any of these pronouns for masculine" rather than what *Ibn Mālik* intended the meaning to be, which is, "use only these pronouns for feminine."

Regrettably, I could not examine the original manuscript of *Alfiyyat Ibn Mālik.* Fortunately though, the text line being discussed is a poem text line; meaning it can easily be checked against the well-known Arabic poetry rhyming scale Arabic typography background with an eye to distinguish and

ميزان الشعر to determine the correct reading. Coming from an understand Arabic letters' shapes, and using the simple fact that *Ibn Mālik* had used *wāw* between *dhī* and *dhih*, I concluded that the puzzling word before *tā* must be another *wāw*, since in Arabic, one cannot add another item to an existing item without using *wa* before. It is my impression that the scribe had simply written a badly executed letter *wāw* with very small loop and long downward stroke, which can easily be confused with final *yā'*. Here is what I believe *Ibn Mālik* poem line said:

بذا لمُفْرَدٍ مُذكـّرٍ أشـرْ   بـذي وذهْ وتا على الأنثى اقتَصرْ

To test if my belief holds any truth, I sent an enquiry to *Sa'dī Yūsuf* (one among the most prominent Arab poets today whom I have the honor to know and befriend). I included in my email five versions of the *Ibn Mālik* poem line, including mine, and asked him which one would be the correct one according to Arabic poem rhyming rules. He replied promptly, stating that the correct one was my version, using *waw* before *tā.* I was not surprised that this would be his answer since *Ibn Manẓūr*, who had studied the most important Arabic grammar books of his time, did not list *tī* as a simple feminine demonstrative pronoun in his dictionary textbook, *Lisān al-'Arab.* [13]

The second reference listed by Bellamy for the word *tī* was page 152 of *Ancient west Arabian*, by Chaim Rabin. [7] Rabin hinted that *tī* was used as a simple feminine demonstrative noun by quoting from *Bukhārī*, who wrote that prophet

Muhammad had addressed *ʿĀʾisha*, his youngest wife, with the phrase *kaifa tīkum* كيف تيكم. Rabin must have thought that using *tī* in the compound demonstrative word *tīkum* would mean that it was also used as an independent simple feminine demonstrative pronoun. Writing his book three decades after the discovery of *al-Namārah*, he then listed the *tī* of *al-Namārah* as second reference! [25] Plainly said, this is wrong and misleading. The *tī* of *tīkum* is derived from *tā*, the classic simple feminine demonstrative pronoun. *Ibn Manẓūr* extensively discussed this topic in his introduction to the letter *tāʾ* in *Lisān al-ʿArab*. He explained that *tā* is the simple feminine demonstrative pronoun and that it can be used as a standalone word to point to a single feminine. He further explained: *Tayyā* is the diminutive demonstrative pronoun of *tā* which can possibly be used for a younger female too. Clearly, when pointing to a single feminine noun as a third distant party, *tā* can be combined to form a new compound demonstrative pronoun, as *tī*, but one cannot use this part as a standalone word. For example, the words *tīka*, and *tilka* are derived from *tā*, not *tī*. The Arabs used *tīka* instead of *tāka*, but some had used *tālika*, instead of *tilka*, which *Ibn Manẓūr* called the ugliest usage in the language. [13]. Other than this occurrence claimed by the readers of *al-Namarāh,* I could not find a single example for using *tī* as a simple feminine demonstrative pronoun, be that in the Quran, Arabic poetry, or anywhere else. Even if one were to find such an example, it would be of a wrong usage and surely a post Islamic example. The three simple feminine demonstrative pronouns in Arabic are *tā, dhī,* and *dhih.*

3.5 Rereading *al-Namārah* Nabataean Arabic Inscription

Taking into account the numerous *Musnad* Arabic inscriptions available today, *al-Namārah* or any of the three other known Nabataean Arabic inscriptions cannot be classified as the earliest Arabic language documents on record. Although the classic Arabic language of *al-Namārah* is truly remarkable, the inscription quality is not impressive. Moreover, the quality of the stone and the efforts put to prepare it, are much higher than the quality of the inscription and the efforts put by the scribe, and most likely, this scribe was definitely not the same person who prepared the stone. Surely, *al-Namārah* stone as a whole does not look like a stone worthy of a king's tomb or monument. Despite visible damages, possibly including a complete breakup of the stone into two or more pieces, most of the words of *al-Namārah* inscription are uncomplicated to read by a person familiar with the Nabataean and Arabic scripts. Out of the several erosions that afflicted the stone, only one or two areas of erosion had somewhat affected the reading of the inscription. Although reading *al-Namārah,* a fascinating archeological and philological task, can be very challenging, it is not very complicated once the first two lines, and particularly the first two words, of the inscription are read correctly. Numerous scholars studied *al-Namārah* after Dussaud, but Professor Bellamy of the University of Michigan should get the highest credit for re-reading *al-Namārah* from scratch and presenting original corrections along with fresh new pictures, in the eighties of last century.

The first time I read *al-Namārah* was in 2008, the year I published my first article about the history of the Arabic *Jazm* script. My involvement in Arabic typography brought me earlier into the field of history of the Arabic script. In my earlier readings, I utilized available pictures and tracings, particularly those provided by Bellamy. With the help of my patient brother who visited the Louvre Museum in 2009, and the aid of the great technology inside his digital camera, I was able to examine the stone *in person* and obtain numerous detailed pictures of the areas disputed by previous readers including myself. I have provided, in Figure 4.4, the original Nabataean tracing of *al-Namārah* by Dussaud, along with his initial Arabic reading as referenced today by most textbooks. Thanks to Hassan Jamil, my ex-student and assistant who taught me Photoshop, I was able to provide my new tracing (Figure 3.5) of *al-Namārah* with eleven new changes —out of the eleven, three are Bellamy's and six are mine. To assist the readers locating these new tracings and compare them with the old ones, I assigned a number to each affected area on Dussaud's original tracing (Figure 3.4.) Also, in Figure 3.5, I provided my own letter-for-letter Arabic transcription followed by my translation into Arabic of the inscription, where I added all necessary dots,

Figure (3.4) A photo of *al-Namārah* stone hanging on a wall at the Louvre Museum, Paris. © Marie-Lan Nguyen / Wikimedia Commons [20]

Dussaud's tracing of al-Namārah Nabataean inscription

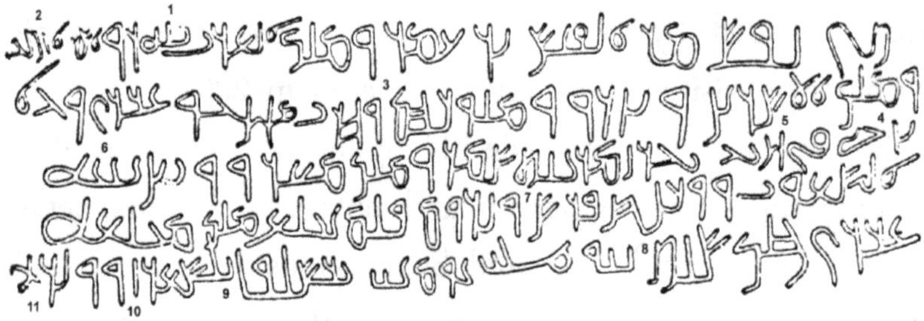

Dussaud's letter-by-letter Arabic transcription and reading

تِى نفسُ امرءِ القيس بر عمرٍو مَلِك العرب كُلّه ذو أَسَرَ التاج

ومَلَكَ الاسدين ونزارو ومُلوكَهم وهَرَّبَ مجو عكدى وجاء

بِزَجاى ڨ حبّج نجران مدينت شمّر ومَلَكَ معدّو وبَيَّنَ بَنيه

الشعوب ووَكَّلَهُنَّ فارِسو لِرُوم فَلَمْ يبلغ مَلِك مبلغَهُ

عكدى هَلَكَ سنت 223 يَوّم 7 بِكسلول بالسعْد ذو وَلَدَهُ

Figure (3.5) Dussaud tracing of *al-Namārah* inscription with his revised letter-for-letter Arabic transcription and translation. [11]

Author's new tracing of *al-Namārah* Nabataean inscription

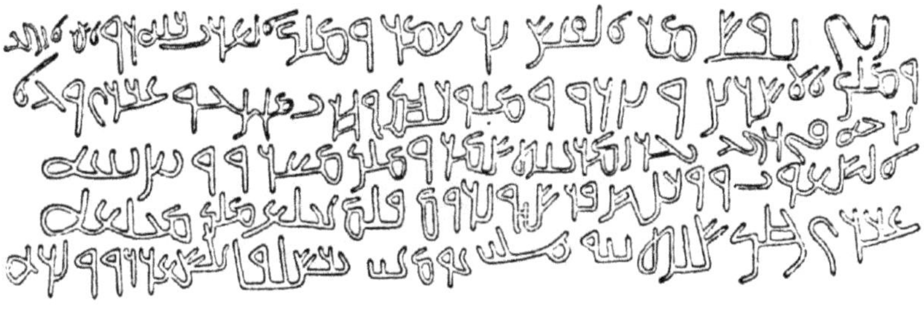

Author's letter-by-letter Arabic transcription

تي نفس مرء لقيس بر عمرو ملك العرب كله ذو اسد التج
وملك الاسدين ونزرو وملوكهمو هرب مذحجو عكدي وجء
يزجه في رتج نجرن مدينت شمرو ملك معدو وبين بنيه
الشعوب ووكلهن فرسنولروم فلم يبلغ ملك مبلغه
عكدي هلك سنت 223 يوم 7 بكسلول يلسعد ذو ولده

Modern Arabic translation with *ailfs,* dots and diacritic vocalization added

تَيا نَفسُ امرؤ القيس بن عَمْرو، مَلِكُ العَربِ كُلِّها، ذو أسَدَ التاج،
ومَلِكُ الأسَديين ونَزارٍ ومُلوكَهُمو. هَرَّبَ مِذْحِج عكْدي، وجاءَ
يزُجُّها في رُتِجِ نَجران، مدينةُ شِمرْ، مَلِكُ مَعَدٍ، وبَيّنَ بَنيها
الشعوب، ووكَّلَهُنَّ فُرْسانو الروم، فَلَمْ يبلغْ مَلِكُ مَبلَغَه.
عكْدي هَلكَ سَنَةَ 223 يَومْ 7 بكسلولْ ، يالِسَعْدِ ذو وَلَدَه.

Figure (3.6) New tracing by the author of the Nabataean text of *al-Namārah* inscription with an equivalent letter-by-letter Arabic transcription and a modern classic Arabic translation.

diacritic vowels, punctuations, and missing letters *alif* in accordance with my new reading. I also provided a full Arabic explanation for my readings. In addition, for those who want to confirm the tracings of this study, I supplied a clear image of the *al-Namārah* stone (Figure 3.3.)

Line 1

Demonstrating that Dussaud's reading of the first word *tī* was inaccurate, would most certainly open the way to question all current readings of the inscription. After all, if the writer of *al-Namārah* inscription had wanted to use a demonstrative pronoun for a tombstone, he would have certainly used *dnh*, the one utilized in *Umm al-Jimāl*, *Raqqush*, and all other Nabataean tombstone inscriptions. Still, in order to fully accomplish the difficult task of challenging Dussaud's reading, we are faced by an even more difficult task — how to read this unusual and difficult word? To begin, I started in Aramaic where *tī* is thought to be a simple demonstrative pronoun for a singular masculine noun. The name of the Syrian village *Tīshūr, Ṭarṭūs* providence, is believed to be derived from an Aramaic compound name made of *tī* (this) and *shūr* (wall), a masculine noun in both Aramaic and Arabic. [3][9]

However, the second word, *nafs*, of *al-Namārah* is a feminine noun — as I have pointed out when re-reading the *Umm al-Jimāl* inscription. The extremely rare instance where *nafs* can be treated as a masculine noun in Arabic is not applicable here. Considering that al-*Namārah* language is relatively classic Arabic, it is seriously unlikely that it would start with an Aramaic word, let alone the wrong Aramaic word.

Regardless of the nature of the word *nafs*, feminine or masculine, one needs to first reinvestigate its meaning and usage in *al-Namārah*. As stated, since this word rarely appeared within the opening phrase of the Nabataean inscriptions but commonly within the Musnad inscriptions of eastern Arabian tombstones (always combined with the word *qabr*), scholars believe this word means "funerary monument". However, no other existing evidence can attest to such common usage among Muslim Arabs. As I illustrated through my reading of the *Umm al-Jimāl*, Madeba, and Stratsbourg inscriptions above, this word was likely misread or even mistraced in these inscriptions. Among the long list of its usage in Arabic (compiled by major Muslim scholars who lived a couple centuries after *al-Namārah*), "tombstone" or "funerary monument" were both clearly absent. Two Arabic Nabataean inscriptions, dated few decades before *al-Namārah* and found in the same geographic area, and numerous other Musnad and Nabataean inscriptions, had consistently used the word *qabr* in relation to a burial place. Why would *al-Namārah* then use *nafs* alone?

Even if the word *nafs* was actually used individually in few inscriptions to mean tombstone, this should certainly not limit it to that usage or exclude others, especially since the absolute majority of the other inscriptions had consistently used it otherwise. The fact that *Umm al-Jimāl* had used *nafsū* with final *wāw,* while *al-Namārah* used *nafs* without *wāw,* is by itself a significant piece of information that needs to be examined closely. Furthermore, *al-Namārah* stone does not even resemble a typical Nabataean or non-Nabataean *nafesh.* I am of the opinion that in the context of *al-Namārah*, the word *nafs* should be read as "soul" — its common usage —, or "blood" — a less common but a very valid usage, given the events surrounding *Umru'ū al-Qays* defeat. As it will be emphasized throughout my re-reading, the overall text contents, paragraphs, sentences, and information on the events cited in the inscription — whether read with classic Arabic or having Nabataean Arabic in mind — do not match the current reading of this word as "funerary monument."

My reading of *nafs* in the meaning of "soul" would leave only a couple of possibilities for the reading of the previous word, *tī.*—it was either used to swear by or call upon the soul or blood of *Umru'ū al-Qays*, a very common Arab practice even today; or to bring the attention to or call upon his glory. It was customary that the Arabs, even before Islam, use introductory sentences before starting with their main topic as Muslims routinely do today by starting with an attention-grabbing swear sentence such as, *Bism Allāh al-Raḥmān al-Raḥīm.* Accordingly, I believe there could be four possible readings for *tī.*

The first and most likely reading of it is *tayā* تَيَا, a combined word composed of two parts, *ta* and *yā.* The first part is the swearing letter *tā'*, known as *tā' al-qasam* تاء القسم, as in *ta-Allāh* تَاللّه. Contrary to common belief today, starting with the swear letter *tā'* was not limited to *Allāh.* For example, the Arabs used *ta-Ḥayātika* تحياتك when swearing by someone's life. They also used *ta-rabbi al-ka'bati* تربّ الكعبة when swearing by the god of *ka'bah* in Mecca— even before Islam. [4][13] Based on this reading, they may have used *tayā rabbi al-Ka'batati* تيا ربّ الكعبة. The second part, the letter/word *yā* is *ḥarf tanbīh* حرف تنبيه commonly used to call, or call upon, the attention of someone or something as in *yā Allāh,* or *yā fulān,* or *yā 'Irāq.* [13] Therefore, I read the first two words of *al-Namārah* as *ta-yā nafs* تيا نفس, as in *qasaman yā nafs* قسما يا نفس, or *bikī yā nafs* بِكِ يا نفس, which would mean, "swear by thee O'soul of", or "in thee, O'soul of."

The second possible reading is that *tī* could also be *tayā* تَيا, but this time the two parts are used together as *ḥarf tanbīh.* *Ibn Manẓūr* listed several examples where *yā,* combined with additional letters before it were used as one word in the meaning of *yā.* The additional letters before *yā* were possibly used to add more emphasis, admiration, or to express feelings for revenge and sorrow. The few examples listed in his *Lisān al-'Arab* included *āyā* آيا, *'ayā* أيا, and *hayā* هيا, but not *tayā* تيا. [13] My thinking, based on *Ibn Manẓūr* examples, is that *tayā* and several other combinations of *yā* had existed in classic Arabic.

The third possibility is that it could actually be *tī* تي, but was used either as a feminine pronoun *hadhihī* هذه in the meaning of *ḥarf tanbīh,* solely to swear and give attention and admiration, or as a swearing letter *tā'* with final letter *yā'* to replace the *kasrah* diacritic. In the latter case, it would be read *tī nafs* as in *bi-nafs* بنفس or *wa-nafs* ونفس, commonly used to swear by someone's soul. Swearing *tā'* is normally attached to a word and used with a *fathah* diacritic, but it is possible that it was given *kasrah* when used with a feminine noun like *nafs*. This is consistent with the typical Arabic association of *kasrah* with feminine. Since pronouncing *ta* with *kasra* when attached to *nafs* is awkward, a final *yā'* was probably used to represent *kasrah*, as practiced in pre-diacritic Arabic poetry writings. [13]

The forth, an extremely unlikely possibility, is that *tī* could also be *tayā*, but in the meaning of *ṭawbá* طوبى or *taḥyā* تحيا (long live.) The inscription may have started with the phrase *taḥyā nafs* تحيا نفس but the *ḥa'* after *tā'* was possibly omitted by design or by mistake. This possibility is highly unlikely since I have not found any evidence linking *tī* or *tayā* with such usage. Also, *taḥyā* is usually used with a living person, not the soul of the dead.

Reading the first two words of *al-Namārah* is crucial to the reading of the rest of the inscription. In the case of the first three reading possibilities here above reported, swearing by or calling upon *Umru'ū al-Qays'* soul, the phrase should then be followed by a single major action or event announcement, not a group of events. As for the fourth possibility, the non-swearing readings above, a list of accomplishments is certainly possible. Regardless of which reading is used, the inscription has become much less likely a burial epitaph than a memorial monument. The first three swearing readings open up other possibilities for reading the rest of the inscription, since they indicate that this inscription is not about *Umru'ū al-Qays.*

The next questionable word of the first line was *klh* Dussaud traced the word as *klh* accurately, but read it wrongly as *kulluh.* It should be *kulluhā* (meaning, "all of them") referring to the previous word *al-'Arab* (the Arabs, or the Arab tribes); both are feminine nouns. However, the next challenging words of the inscription are *dhū* and the two words following it. As I explained earlier, in Arabic *dhū* is usually used in the meaning of *ṣāḥib* or *wa-lahu* ("owner of" or "he who owns"), normally for *laqab* or *kunyah* (last name), or in the meaning of "who or which belongs to", or "of". In both cases, it should be followed by a noun. However, in classic Arabic, *dhū* was also used in the meaning of *alladhī* (he who), followed by a verb. In *al-Namārah*, the next word was either *asad* (lion) or *asara* (took someone as prisoner). I believe it was the noun *asad*, and the previous word was either *dhū,* normally used for nicknames or other titles, or *dhū* in the meaning of "who belogs to", not *alladhī.*

It follows, I read the last three-word phrase as *dhū asadu al-tāj* in the meaning of "the one who owned *asad al-tāj*," possibly a nickname or title referring to a figure of lion adorning the top of an actual crown. Or in the meaning of "the one who belongs to *asadu al-tāj*". This refers to the *Asad* tribe as the one with the crown or the one whose kings wore a crown, a well-known history fact.

In order to read *dhū* as *alladhī*, to fulfill Dussaud's and all current readings of the inscription, one must read the word after *dhū* as a verb. Scholars, who read the word after *dhū* as a verb, possibly *asara*, *assara*, or even *asada*, claimed that the word which followed and which can easily be traced as the noun *al-tāj* (crown,) was actually referring to the well-known historical city *Thāj* or *Tha'j* near the modern-day city *al-Ḍahrān*.

Even so, if this were true, one would not refer to it as *al-Thāj* using *al*. In fact, Arabic poetry had never used *al* with city names like *Thāj* or *Najrān*. Additionally, in Arabic the object of the verb *asar* or *assara* must be people, not a city. One does take people, particularly soldiers, as prisoners and not a city! Tweaking the reading of *al-tāj*, some scholars claimed it was actually *al-Tājiyyīn*, possibly a tribe name, or *al-Thājiyyīn*, the people of the city of *Thāj*. However, I was not able to trace the two or three additional letters needed for *al-tāj* to become *al-Tājiyyīn* or *al-Thājiyyīn*. Since those who read the word as the verb *assara* had also read each subsequent word *mlk* as the verb *malaka*, one may ask as why *al-Namārah* would use *assar* only for *al-Taj* or *al-Tājiyyīn*. A more pertinent question would be, why not use *malaka*? It would certainly fit the meaning better.

Those who opposed reading *al-tāj* as "the crown" explained that Arab kings had never wore crowns. This is erroneous. History teaches us that some of the northern Arab kings of *Ḥīrah* and even *Najd,* home of the *Bani Asad* tribes, wore crowns. Even if this were not true, we do know that *Umru'ū al-Qays* had carried many attacks in Persia whose kings did wear crowns. Since Persia historically used a lion as a national symbol, we cannot exclude the possibility that *Umru'ū al-Qays* had managed to seize a crown with a lion effigy — this earned him the appellation: *dhū asad al-tāj* (the one with the lion of the crown), a valid Arabic phrase in terms of grammar and semantics. According to Muslim scholars, King *Umru'ū al-Qays* was known for his many appellations. Doing so, that is to have multiple nicknames, is an established Arab tradition since time immemorial, through the Abbasid times, and even today. One would be surprised, if *al-Namārah* would mention king *Umru'ū al-Qays* without following it with one of his many titles or appellations. It is unfortunate that the appellation listed in *al-Namārah* was not among those that Muslim historians accorded to him. [14][30]

Struggling to read the word following *dhū* as a verb to prove Dussaud's general classification of *al-Namārah,* some scholars hypothesized that *assar* was an equivalent to the verb *nāla* (won). They read the second word as "is"; that is, as *al-tāj* (crown), and read the three-word phrase as *alladhi nāla al-tāj* (he who won the crown). Yet, I found no evidence that *assara* or *asara* was used in such manner.

Bellamy read the last four-word phrase as *wa-laqabahu dhū Asad wa-Midhḥij* (and his appellation as "the one who owned *Asad* and *Midhḥij* tribes".) I do agree with his tracing of the loop following *Asad* as possible letter *wāw*, but disagree with his tracing of the word that followed as *Midhḥij*. Doubly important, why would *al-Namārah* lists *Umru'ū al-Qays'* as king of *Asad* and vanquisher of *Midhḥij* in Line 2 (according to Bellamy's reading) when his appellation already included them on Line 1? However, I believe Bellamy's tracing of *alif* as possible *wāw* would change *dhū asad al-tāj* ذو اسد التاج to *dhū asadūl-tāj* ذو اسدولتاج which would conform to the way with which *al-Namārah* pronounced the name *Umru'ū al-Qays* as *Umru'ul-Qays* مرء لقيس and, as I shall discuss later, the way it pronounced *fursān al-Rūm* as *fursanūl-rūm* فرسانولروم. On the other hand, even if all Bellamy's tracing and reading of the last phrase of Line 1 were correct, this would still agree with my reading of *dhū* as the common *dhū* and not *alladhī*, and with my reading of the phrase as one of the king's titles or appellations.

Line 2

Reading the first two and the last three words of the first line was, without a doubt, the most demanding task in reading the Arabic language of *al-Namārah*. In comparison, reading the rest of the inscription is straightforward. If *dhū* was *alladhī*, one would expect a series of action (i.e. verbs) afterwards, all connected by *wa* (and). If it was simply the typical word *dhū* for appellations, one should then expect either additional titles connected by *wa*, or an announcement for an extraordinary event or a decree. Only in the second case could one start a new sentence with the letter *wāw* (not in the meaning "and"), which would normally be followed by a non-verb, as in *wa-qad*, or *wa-akīran*. The fact that *Umru'ū al-Qays* was the king of *Asad* and *Nazār*, is neither new nor an extraordinary announcement. The Quran stated many sentences with *wāw*, but it consistently used non-verb afterwards, as in the example of Quran (53:1) *wa-al-najmi idhā hawá* والنّجمِ إذا هوى, where the word *al-najm* (the star) is a noun.

In my opinion, reading the word *mlk,* which appears twice in the second line, as the verb *malaka* is a major mistake since the first one was preceded by the letter *wāw*. I read both as the noun *malik* (king of), as this same word was read by all scholars in Line 1 in the phrase *malik al-'Arab*. Muslim scholars wrote that *banī Asad* of *Najd* and *banī Nazar* of *Ḥijāz*, are *'Arabun musta'ribah* (Arabized Arabs), not *'Arabun 'āribah* (pure Arabs.) They are the descendants of *'Adnān*, not *Qaḥṭān* (presumably a "pure" Arab.) Accordingly, *'Adnān*, a descendent of *Isma'īl*, is the father (some wrote grandfather) of *Nazār* of *Ḥijāz* and *Ma'ad of* Yemen, and great grandfather of *Muḍar.* Depending on what time period, these mixed Arab groups were customarily referred to as *Ma'ad, Nazār*, or *Muḍar* instead of *'Adnān.* [2][28] It is evident, therefore, that after stating that *Umru' al-Qays* was the king of all Arabs — the single largest group of people in the area — the writer of *al-Namārah* needed to state that *Umru'ū al-Qays* was also the king of both *Asad* and *Nazār*, two of the largest three mixed tribes in Arabia. The third group is *Ma'ad* of Yemen. Yet, it is also possible that the term "all Arabs" was referring to all nomadic Arab tribes as distinguished from tribes that had settled down in cities and specific geographic areas and established kingdoms.

Based on my readings of the word *malik* above as noun, I had suspected right from the begining, that the letter *wāw* after the next word, *mulūkahum,* should actually be a part of that word. This would make reading Arabic smoother, especially since the next word, *h.r.b* is a definite verb, as we shall see that later. This, of course, was not required for my reading of *al-Namārah* up to the word *mulūkahum.* As explained above, a sentence announcing an extraordinary event, like defeating the powerful *Midhḥij*, can start with *wāw* in the meaning of *wa-akīran* (at last or finally), or *hā-qad.* However, tracing and inspecting the Nabataean text, I can unmistakably see that the *wāw* after *mulūkahum* is actually connected to it. The downward stroke of this *wāw* is not vertical. It is pointing to the right. The final letter *mīm* of *mulūkahum* has a prominent lower-connecting stroke fading just before it reaches the downward stroke of *wāw.* I read this word as *mulūkahumū* not *mulūkahum.* This final *wāw* is referring to the people of *Asad* and *Nazār.* In Arabic grammar, it is called *wāw al-Ishba'* (saturation *wāw*) or *wāw al-ṣilah* (*relating wāw*) and is usually used after *mīm al-Jam'* (plural *mīm*) to emphasize its *dhammah* diacritic. The word *mulūkahumū* is the last word of the opening sentence of *al-Namārah.* It does not only conclude the opening sentence in anticipation of the main subject of the inscription, but it surely makes the reading of the first word of *al-Namārah, tī,* as “this”, impossible.

The Arabic root of the word after *mulūkahumū* could either be *haraba* هرب (run away) or *hadhdhaba* هذّب (disciplined), a verb in both cases. Tracing this word as *hrb* is accepted by all scholars. Since the word that comes after was *Midhḥij*, the name of the prominent Yemenite tribe, this verb must be in past tense and when read in Arabic must have a *shaddah* on the letter *rā’* to become *harraba* هرّب (forced the object to run away) in order to refer to the subject committing the action of the verb. If *Midhḥij* is the object, as I read it, the subject can then be a name appearing before or after the verb. The only other possibility is to treat *Midhḥij*, a feminine noun, as the subject, not the object of the verb; in such case, one must say *harabat Midhḥij*, adding the feminine letter *tā’* after *bā’*. Since there was no *tā’*, this word must be *harraba* (defeated them or made them run away.) *Hadhdhaba* would not make sense after reading the next line.

Given that *harraba* was the first word of the new main event announcing a sentence/paragraph that followed an unrelated opening sentence, and since it was definitely a verb followed by a name within a three-word sub-sentence, the next word *‘Akdī* عكْدي must be the subject name according to classic Arabic. It cannot be an adjective or adverb since this would leave the three-word sub-sentence incomplete. I agree with Dussaud's reading of the phrase as *harraba Midhḥij ʿAkdī*, but I read it in the meaning of the phrase *harraba ʿAkdī Midhḥij*, where *ʿAkdī* is the subject فاعل who defeated the object مفعول به *Midhḥij*. In Arabic, one can use both phrases, but should differentiate between them by using appropriate vocal accents on the object and subject. This vocal differentiation was never marked in writing until after Islam. The Quran and Arabic poetry have plenty of similar examples. In the Quran (35:28) *innamā yakhshá Allāha min ʿibadihi al-ʿulamaʾu* إِنَّمَا يَخْشَى اللَّهَ مِنْ عِبَادِهِ الْعُلَمَاءُ, where the verb *yakhshá* is the first word followed immediately by *Allāh*, the object, and then comes the subject, *al-ʿulamaʾu*.[18][19]

However, assuming that *ʿAkdī* was a name in the phrase *harraba Midhḥij ʿAkdī*, one should also consider the possibility that *Midhḥij* was a personal name and is the subject. In such case, *ʿAkdī*, as the object, would be the personal or tribe name of the defeated party. Although this possibility is valid from a grammar and language angle, it would not fit at all with all readings of the last line of the inscription where the victorious (either *ʿAkdī*, or *Umrūʾ al-Qays*) was treated as a hero, not a villain. Similarly, the assumption that *ʿAkdī* was a last name, as in *haraba Midhḥij ʿAkdī*, would not work with the rest of the inscription.

Luckily, from the viewpoint of research, the word *ʿAkdī* appeared twice in the inscription. The last sentence started with the two-word phrase *'Akdī halak* (*'Akdī* died.) This phrase is, by itself, solid proof that *'Akdī* is a name of a person and that this inscription is about him, not *Umru'ū al-Qays.* The main event of the inscription was his triumph over *Midhḥij.* Not a very common name, *'Akdī* sounds like a classic Arabic name. Many of Arabic names are formed by adding final *yā'* after a noun or after another name derived from a three-letter Arabic root, as in *Ramzī* from *Ramz, Sa'dī* from *Sa'd, Ḥusnī* from *Ḥusn,* ... etc. The name of the hero of *al-Namarāh* was *'Akdī* derived from the classic Arabic word *'akd* عكد. It is that simple! With a simple Arabic Google search for the name *'Akdī,* one can find many using it as a last name in an Arab desert town in Algeria, called *Umāsh* أوماش ! The fact that the name *'Akdī* was mentioned without the name of his father could mean that he was either an associate of *Umru'ū al-Qays,* from a slave background like the famous Arab hero *'Antarah* (who many think was originally a slave) or a high ranking Arab soldier of the Roman Army.

According to *Lisān al-'Arab,* although the root word *'akd* can be used in a variety of meanings; however, its primary meaning is, "the lower back part of the tongue." For that reason, it was used in the meaning of *aṣl* (origin) as Libzbarski suggested. The word is probably related to *'iqd* عِقد (tie). [7][13] Likely, the derived word *'akdi* does not mean "strong" or "powerful", as most Arabic publications desperately claim today following Caskel's reading, but "original" اصلي. Besides, one can not see how anyone could read the same word *Akdī* in two ways at the same time: as "the strong" القوي, and "with strength or strongly" قوّتاً!

Bellamy thought this word was *ʿakkaḍá* عكضى, which he desperately tried to make derive from a two-word phrase *ʿan kaḍá* عن قضى with the letter *nūn* assimilated, the letter *qāf* replaced, and the letter *yāʾ* ignored. He thought this word meant "thereafter". [7] His reading of the word as an adverb would make sense if one would go along with Dussaud's reading of the previous text. But even then, his convoluted assumptions to arrive to this unknown word, *ʿakkaḍá*, raise more questions but give no answers. For example, why can't an inscription, with relatively good classic Arabic language, use *baʿda dhālik,* instead? Why is there no reference to *ʿan kaḍá,* as "thereafter" in any historical Arabic reference? In the first place, why would the writer of the inscription use a non-crucial adverb twice?

Line 3

Bellamy should be given due credit for tracing and reading two higly debated words in the beginning of Line 3. I verified his tracing and I agree with it. He traced the first word as *yzjh* and read it *yazujjuhā.* The missing final *alif* after *hāʾ* is consistent with the word *kulluh* for *kulluhā* in Line 1 and with another word *banīh* for *banīhā,* in the end of Line 3. *Yazujju* has many meanings, but in *al-Namārah* context, it means, "to engage someone in a fierce battle." Dussaud traced that word as *bzji* and read it as *bi-zjāy*, a non-existing Arabic word! The second traced word by Bellamy was *rtj*, which he read as *rutuji* in the meaning of "gates of". I agree with his tracing of the word, but disagree with his Arabic reading and the meaning he gave to it. The presence of *fī* (in) rather than *'alá* (on) before the word indicates that it does not mean gates in this context. The word *fī* (in) needs a location where one can be physically "in" not "near to". One cannot say in Arabic *fī abwāb Najrān* (in the gates of *Najrān*), but *'alá abwāb Najrān* (on/at the gates of *Najrān*.) I read the word *rtj* as *rutuji,* or possibly *ritāji,* in the meaning of "narrow roads of" or "narrow road of" as given by *Lisān al-'Arab*, which indicated that the words *rutuj* or *marātij* are the plural forms of the word *ritāj* for "narrow road", as in the Quran verse وأرض ذات رتاج.[13]

Categorically therefore, only this reading is grammatically correct as it is in agreement with the historical and geographical facts of *Najrān* and Yemen, which are known for their narrow roads and mountainous valleys. The use of the word *harraba* in the second line was apparently deliberate. The crushing battle was in and around *Najrān,* where *Midhḥij* had escaped to for cover. Further, scholars read the word *Shimr* as *Shammar*, probably hinting to the well-known *Shammar* tribe of northern *Najd*. Reading the word as a tribe name rather than an individual name is clearly influenced by reading the following word *mlk* as the verb *malaka*. This hasty reading is yet another example of how scholars did all they can do to prove that *al-Namārah* was listing *Umru'ū al-Qays* accomplishments.

Two facts attest to the following conclusion: 1) geographically, in the sense of distance and location, the *Shammar* tribe had nothing to do with *Najrān* or Yemen, and 2) a renowned king of Yemen who ruled in the time of *al-Namārah* carried the first name *Shimr.* [2][6][14] Moreover, I wonder why *al-Namārah*, which had added *wāw* after every single name in the inscription, would skip that practice only with the name *Shammar!* I read the word *Shmr* and the *wāw* that followed as one word, *Shimrū*, referring to King *Shimr Yar'ish* of Yemen, and therefore, I read the next word that followed as *mālik* (king of), not the verb *malaka* (owned).

The last two words of the third line are *wa-bayyana banīhā*, as in *wa mayyaza bayna banīhā* (distinguished appropriately between its people). Bellamy read the two words as *wa-nabala bi-nabahi* (treated its nobles gently). His reading would fit fine with his and my reading of the fourth line, which included two important words, *al-shu'ūb* followed by *wa-wakkalahunna.* For a victorious army, discriminating between the defeated (as in treatment of women, children, and elders differently) is contrary to the usual indiscriminate rampage. In other words, it is a sort of gentle treatment reserved for the vanquished. Tracing the first word by Bellamy as *nbl,* which he read as *nabala,* is possible. Conversely, tracing the second word as *bnbh,* which he read as *bi-nabahi* is impossible since the third letter is clearly *yā',* not *bā'.* I read the first word as *bayyana*, as did Dussaud even though the vertical stem of the final letter nūn was unusually high.

In Arabic *bayyana* in the meaning of *mayyaza* (distinguished between) or in the meaning of *wadhdhaḥa* (clarified) is the past tense for *yubayyin*. Among many diverse modes of usage, the Quran (2:118) used the following: قَدْ بيـنّا الآيَاتِ لِقَوْمٍ يـُوقِـنُون. The root word, *bayn* is among the few Arabic words that can be used to give an opposite meaning. Generally, it is used to express either separation or togetherness.[13] As for the second word, I believe it is *banīhā*, as in *abnā'ihā* (its sons or people). The word *bnh* should be read as *banīhā*, since we are referring either to the *Midhḥij* tribe or *to Ma'ad*, both of which are feminine nouns. Dussaud read this word, *banyihi*, as in *quwwatihi* (his steadfastness). This would fit well with the rest, but it needs to be followed by *lil-shu'ūb*, not *al-shu'ūb* as illustrated in the next word of Line 4.

Line 4

The fourth line presents no obstacles to read. In the beginning, Dussaud read it correctly, but a few decades later, he reversed position. The word *wwklhn* should be read *wa-wakkalahunna* (put them under the protection of), a classic Arabic word that is grammatically correct.[13] As it happened, *al-Namārah* included the required letter *nūn* with *shaddah* at the end, which is needed to refer specifically to the plural feminine noun *al-shu'ūb.* This word is the second widely-utilized taxonomic term used in the Arab tribal and modern systems as synonym for the word "people". A tribe or *qabīlah* is divided into *shuʿūb,* plural for *shaʿb,* which in turn is divided into *buṭūn.* We read in the Quran (9:36) إِنَّ عِدَّةَ الشُّهُورِ عِندَ اللَّهِ اثْنَا عَشَرَ شَهْرًا فِي كِتَابِ اللَّهِ يَوْمَ خَلَقَ السَّمَاوَاتِ وَالأَرْضَ مِنْهَا أَرْبَعَةٌ حُرُمٌ ذَلِكَ الدِّينُ الْقَيِّمُ فَلَا تَظْلِمُواْ فِيهِنَّ أَنفُسَكُمْ. The word *fīhhunna* فيهن is referring to the plural feminine word *shuhūr* (months); therefore the letter *nūn*, known as *nūn al-niswah* نون النسوة (feminine *nūn*) — used to make feminine plural nouns — must be added in the end. [18][19] The word *shahr* (month) is a single masculine noun, but when converted to plural form, it becomes *shuhūr*, a feminine noun. Similarly, the word *shuʿūb*, plural of the masculine noun *shaʿb*, is a plural feminine noun. The rules for *nūn al-niswah* explain, partially, why the word *al-ʿArab*, a single feminine noun, in the first line was referred to with *kulluhā*, not *kulluhunna* or *kullahum,* and why the feminine noun, *Midhḥij*, for a single tribe, was referred to with the words, *yazujjuhā*, not *yazujuhunna* or *yazujuhum*, and *banīhā* not *banīhunna,* or *banīhum.*

The contested word(s) of the fourth line was *frswlrwm.* The first three-letter part *frs* can be *faras* (horse), *fāris* (horseman or equestrian), or *Fāris* (Persia). Reading the word as "horse" cannot be considered. To read history correctly, it is literally impossible for the word to be read as Persia and that is because the previous word was clearly *wa-wakkalahunna*, and the following word was clearly indicating the Romans (there has never been an incidence in old Arabia where an area was put under the simultaneous protection of the Romans and the

Persians.) During the time of *al-Namārah*, found in a Roman-controlled territory, these two powers were engaged in heated battles. Consequently, it was highly improbable to share domination of Arabia as partners.

At this point, we are left with only one possibility as how to read *frsw*, which is *fursānū* (horsemen) plural of *fāris*. I am inclined to believe there is a medial *nūn* between the letters *sīn* and *wāw*, which I will discuss in detail later. Accordingly, I read the two words as a compound: *fursānūl-rūm*, فرسانولروم, for *fursān al-Rūm*, فرسانُ الروم, similar to the reading of *Umru'ul-qays* مرءُ لقيس earlier in the inscription for *Umru' ū al-Qays* أمرؤُ القيس. The *alif* of *al-Rūm* was omitted because it was preceded by a word ending with the letter *wāw*, namely *fursānū*. This practice has largely fallen out of use in modern Arabic writing. The name *Umrū' al-Qays*, is pronounced with heavy *dhammah* accent (as if there was a letter *wāw*) after *hmazah* as in *Umru'ū-l-qays* أمرءُولقيس or *Umru'u-l-qays* أمرءُ لقيس. This is why the beginning letter *alif* of *al-Qays*, not same as *hamzah*, was also omitted. In fact, in modern Arabic, a majority of people write the name with *wāw* beneath *hamzah* as in *Umru'ū al-Qays* أمرؤُ القيس. Some still write it as *'Umru'u al-qays* أمرءُ القيس. In comparison, the *alif* of *al* is not omitted when the previous word ends with a soft *dhammah* diacritic, like *maliku al-Asadiyyin* in the second line. The letter *wāw* after the *nūn* in *fursānū* could be the plural *wāw* normally seen when a perfect masculine plural noun ending with *wāw* and *nūn*, is added to another noun to complete its meaning, as in *banū Asad* for *banūn Asad.* This is known as *jamʿ al-mudhakkar al-sālim* جمع المذكر السالم. The word *fursān* is called *mudhāf* مضاف (qualified) or translated literary from Arabic "the added word," while *al-Rūm* is *mudhāf ilayh* مضاف اليه (qualifier) or translated literally from Arabic "the word which has been added to." Otherwise, this *wāw* could also be *wāw al-ṣilah* or *wāw al-ishbāʿ* to emphasize the *ḍammah* diacritic on the *nūn*, as explained earlier when discussing the word *mulūkahumū* in Line 2.

Dussaud, who initially read the word *frsw* as *fārisū* (plural for *fāris*?), appeared not convinced of his reading. This explains why he decided to get rid of that reading later (when he re-read *al-Namārah* in the 1950s.) A justification does exist to explain this obvious confusion: the area of the stone occupied by the letters *frsw* appears significantly damaged. However, all what the word needs to become *fursānū* is the letter *nūn* between the letters *sīn* and *wāw.*

Fortunately, we do not need to dream up the letter *nūn.* Retracing that area extensively by using several photos, I observed that the down stroke of the letter *wāw* was pointing to the right, not perfectly vertical as traced by Dussaud. More important, the downward stroke of the previous letter *sīn* is clearly making an upward u-turn, probably to form the small missing letter, medial *nūn*, which was then connected to the letter *wāw* just at the loop area. Furthermore, the space between the letters *sīn* and *wāw* is suspiciously wide. Nevertheless, and given that this particular surface is severely damaged, we may never know for sure if there was ever a letter *nūn* in that area of the inscription.

I believe my reading of *frsw* as *fursānū* is more convincing than Dussaud's. It is surely more convincing than Bellamy's reading of it as *fa-ra'asū* فرأسو (to appoint someone as their head or leader.) He read the two-word phrase *fa-ra'asū li-Rūmā.* I cannot see how he traced *hamzah* between the tightly spaced letters *rā'* and *sīn. Hamza,* unlike *alif,* cannot be omitted in this case since *al-Namārah* used it consistently everywhere else. Bellamy's reading seems acceptable at first; but it would quickly crumple when combined with the previous word *wa-wakkalahunna* (placed them under the protection of.) According to Bellamy's reading, the defeated *Midhḥij,* were put under the protection of the defeater (*Umru' al-Qays*), and then accepted the Romans as their ultimate protectors. Why would an Arab king work so hard for the benefit of the Romans? The Arab kings were never enthusiastically subservient to either the Romans or the Persians. Their relation was primarily for mutual protection. [6] Bellamy's elaboration on the differences between *ra'īs* and *malik* is not convincing. Also, his reading of the last word as the city *Rūmā* روما is confusing. Even though the Arabs called the Byzantine Romans *al-Rūm*, these Romans were not the Romans of *Roma* (current Rome of Italy). Why *al-Namārah* would then speak of *Rūmā*?

We have no clue as to how and why some readers read the word *wwklhn* as *wa-kullahum* in order to read the whole phrase as *wa-kullahum fursānan lil-Rūm* (and made all of them knights for the Romans). This highly speculative reading discards arbitrarily one of the two letters *wāw* and dreams up a final letter *mīm*, to replace the letter *nūn,* in *wwklhn.* Additionally, it adds a letter *nūn* after *sīn* (as I did) and replaces the *wāw* by *alif tanwīn* in *frsw.* It also adds, arbitrarily, a second letter *lām* before *lrum.* This and other peculiar readings are unfortunately the most popular ones in the Arab world today; probably because the current major Western readings of *al-Namārah* have failed to convince many! [27]

The last phrase of Line 4, *fa-lam yablugh malikun mablaghah,* which was read that way by all scholars, is clear but tricky. It can mean, "Not even a king could accomplish what he has accomplished" or "no other king has accomplished what he has accomplished". There is a subtle difference between these two interpretations. The second could lead the reader to believe that it is referring to the only king mentioned in *al-Namārah*, king *Umru'ū al-Qays.* I beg to differ; that is, it refers to the first interpretation of the first phrase — that is, the one referring to the accomplishments of *'Akdī.* It is worth mentioning that it is common in the usages of the Arabic to brag about something by stating, "not even a king has done such or had owned such." As I have explained already, according to history textbooks before Dussaud's reading of *al-*

Namārah, king *Umru'ū al-Qays* was not able to control Yemen or *Midhḥij*.

To summarize, the third and fourth lines of *al-Namārah* are describing the sole event of the inscription, namely the defeat of *Midhḥij*, which was introduced in Line 2. Their specific purpose appears to be informing the reader about where the battle took place, how it was conducted, and what was its aftermath. All of the keywords appearing in the two lines, *Midhḥij*, *Najrān*, *al-shu'ūb*, *malik*, *Shimr*, and *al-Rūm* are linked to one geographical location: Yemen, and to a single timeframe: circa 328 CE.

To continue, I read the single event paragraph starting by the word *harraba* (in Line 2) until the end of the Line 4 as follows: "*'Akdī* defeated *Midhḥij*, then engaged them in a fierce battle in the narrow road(s) of *Najrān*, the city of *Shimr*, the king of *Ma'ad*, and separated its people as it fits before placing them under the protection of the Roman cavalry, a task that not even a king had accomplished before." This reading is by no means speculative. I based it on historical and geographical facts— especially on the linguistic aspects of the inscription itself.

Line 5

The final line of *al-Namārah* started with the word *'Akdī*, which we have already discussed (and seen) when we read the second line. Starting with this word in the final line was not a coincidence. The letters of the final word of the previous line, *mablaghahu*, were exaggerated in size and a generous space was left blank after it. It seems, therefore, that the scriber deliberately wanted to start the conclusive sentence in a new line. Starting with the name *ʿAkdī*, he wanted to remind the reader, once more, that the inscription was about him. The second word after *ʿAkdī* was clearly *halaka* (perished) therefore, the first phrase of the sentence was *ʿAkdī halaka* (*ʿAkdī* perished) The subject name here is after the verb, exactly as it was in the older Arabic Nabataean inscription, *Raqqūsh*, which had used the phrase *hiya halakat* (she perished). [11] In good classic Arabic, the verb is usually placed *before* the subject, but this is not required for correct Arabic grammar.

After stating the year, month, and day of his death, the scriber concluded the inscription (according to Dussaud) with the phrase "*bil-saʿd dhū waladahu.*" In Arabic language terms, this interpretation is incomprehensible. That is, we cannot understand it in Arabic. Nor can we understand "*yā-la-saʾdi dhū wālawhu*" meaning, "O', happiness for those who followed him" according to Bellamy. Going further, I agree with Dussaud's tracing, except for the first letter, which he read as *bāʾ*, not *yāʾ*, as Bellamy did. One can easily see that the stroke for the letter *bāʾ* was a vertical straight line throughout the inscription, unlike the stroke for the initial *yāʾ*, which had always included a little dent. I am unable to see the second *wāw* of *wālawhu* that Bellamy traced with the intention to replace the letter *dāl* of *wldh*. It is my judgment that Bellamy's reading of this word was clearly influenced by the assumption that *al-Namārah* was King *Umru'ū al-Qays'* epitaph. We read the last phrase as *yā li-sa'di dhū waladah* (O', the happiness of those who gave birth to him). The first word is the letter *yā* known as *yā' al-tanbīh* (exclamation calling upon for either attention or admiration.) This is the same as the*yā* of *tayā*, the first word of *al-Namārah*. It is used here to draw attention to the word *sa'd* (happiness). Unlike the earlier *dhū* in the first line, *dhū* in this phrase was followed by a verb *waladahu* (gave birth to him), and therefore it is used in the meaning of *alladhī* (those who). The closing phrase should be read in the meaning of "Oh, how happy should his parents be," a classic and familiar line used even today when bringing the bad news of a fallen young soldier, not a king, to his parents!

3.6 Conclusion

For more than a century, it was assumed that *al-Namārah* stone, which Dussaud discovered in 1901 (it is hanging today on a wall in the Louvre Museum in Paris,) was the tombstone of one of the most important pre-Islamic Arab kings, King *Umru'ū al-Qays bin 'Amrū*. My tracing and reading of the inscription suggests that such an assumption (based on Dussaud's initial reading) is inaccurate. In fact, by rereading *al-Namārah* and the two other known fully Arabic Nabataean inscriptions, according to Western scholars, *Raqqūsh* and *Umm al-Jimāl*, I found out that *al-Namārah* inscription was actually about a previously unknown military or tribal person named *ʿAkdī*, who, while working with or under the Roman Byzantine army, managed to defeat the powerful *Midhḥij* tribe of Yemen in the early 4th century. The inscription included only three parts: an opening introductory sentence swearing by the soul of king *Umruʾū al-Qays bin ʿAmrū*, a long paragraph detailing the specifics of *ʿAkdī*'s accomplishments in a single battle, and a closing sentence announcing *ʿAkdī*'s death.

Below is my modern Arabic translation and explanation of the *al-Namārah* inscription:

تَيا (قَسماً يا ؛ يا) نَفسُ (روحُ ؛ دَمُ) امرؤ القيس بن عَمْرو، مَلِكُ العَربِ كلُّها، ذو أسَد التاج (كُنية)، ومَلِكُ الأسَديين (نَجْدْ) ونَزارٍ (بنو نَزار، الحجاز) ومُلوكَهُمُ. (لقد) هَرَّبَ مِذْحِجِ (قبيلة يمانية) عكْدي (اسم قائد)، وجاءَ (اي عكْدي) يزُجُّها (يُقاتلها بضراوة) في رُتِجِ (طُرُقْ ضَيِّقة) نَجران، مدينة شِمرْ (شِمْرْ يَرعشْ)، مَلِكُ مَعَدٍ (بنو مَعَدْ)، وبَيّنَ (مَيّزَ بَيْنَ) بَنيها الشعوب (فروع قبيلة مذْحج)، ووكَّلَهُنّ (وضَعَهُنَّ تحت حماية) فُرْسانُ الروم، فلَمْ يبلغْ مَلِكٌ (اي حتّى مَلِكُ) مَبلَغَه (ما بلَغَهُ عكدي). عكْدي هلَكَ (مات ؛ قُتلَ) سنَةَ 223 (328م)، يَومْ 7 بكسلولْ (كانون الاول)، يالِسَعْدِ (يالسعادةِ) ذو (الذي) ولَدَه (أنْجَبَهُ).

And the following is my reading of the inscription translated to English:

> In thee O' soul of *Umruʾū al-Qays bin ʿAmrū*, king of all Arabs, holder of the crown lion, and king of *al-Asadiyyin* and *Nazār* and their kings. *ʿAkdī* has defeated *Midhḥij* en-

gaging it in a heated battle in the narrow roads of *Najrān*, city of *Shimr*, king of *Ma'ad*, and befittingly differentiated between its people and placed them under the protection of the Roman cavalry — not even a king could accomplish what he had accomplished. *'Akdī* died on December 7th, 223 AD, O' the happiness of those who gave birth to him.

Bibliography

1. Abulhab, Saad D. "Roots of the Arabic script: from Musnad to Jazm. Two Parts." *Dahish Voice* 13, no. 2: 23-32 (2007) & no. 3: 20-29 (2009.)
2. ʿAlī, Jawād. *Tarīkh al-ʿArab qabla al-Islam*. Baghdad: al-Mujammaʿ al-ʿIlmī al-ʿIrāqī, 1959.
3. Assyrian Information Management. *Aramaic Lexicon and Concordance*. http://www.atour.com/dictionary/
4. Bazrāwī, Bāsil. "al-Tāʾ fī al-Lughah al-ʿArabiyyah: Khaṣaʾisuhā al-ṣawtiyyah wa-Istikhdāmātihā." http://pulpit.alwatanvoice.com
5. Beeston, A. F. L. "Languages of Pre-Islamic Arabia." *Arabica,* June-September: 178-186.
6. Beeston, Alfred Felix L. "Pre-Islamic Arabia to the 7th Century AD." Encyclopedia Britannica, Academic Edition. http://www.britannica.com/EBchecked/topic/31568/history-of-Arabia/45972/Himyarites#ref484255
7. Bellamy, James A. "A new Reading of al-Namārah Inscription." *Journal of the American Oriental Society* 105 (1985): 31-48.
8. al-Fawzān, ʿAbd Allāh bin Ṣāliḥ. *Dalīl al-Sālik ilá Alfiyyat bin Mālik*. al-Maktabah al-ʿIlmiyyah. http://Alfuzan.islamlight.net

9. Ḥaṭṭāb, Muḥammad Jamīl. *Muʿjam Maʾānī Asmāʾ al-Mudun wa-al-Qurá fī Muḥāfaẓat Ṭarṭūs.* al-Lādhiqiyyah: Dār al-Mirsāh lil-Ṭibāʿah wa-al-Nashir wa-al-Tawzīʿ, 2008.
10. Healey, J. F and Dhuyayb, Sulaymān ibn ʿAbd al-Raḥmān. *The Nabataean Tomb Inscriptions of Mada'in Salih.* London: Oxford University Press, 1993.
11. Healey, J. F. and Smith, G.R. "The Earliest Dated Arabic Document 267 AD." *Atlal: The Journal of Saudi Arabian Archaeology.* 12 (1989): 77-84.
12. Ibn Mālik, Jamāl al-Dīn bin Muḥammad bin ʿAbd Allāh. *Alfiyyat Ibn Mālik.* al-Maktabah al-Ḥurrah. http://ar.wikisource.org/wiki/
13. Ibn Manẓūr, Abū al-Faḍl Jamāl al-Dīn Muḥammad bin Mukarram. *Lisān al-ʿArab.* http://www.islamweb.net/newlibrary/
14. al-Khawārizmī. *Muftāh al-ʿŪlūm.* al-Bāb al-Sādis, fī al-ʾAkhbār. al-Maktabah al-Ḥurrah. http://ar.wikisource.org/wiki/
15. Lendering, Jona. "*Sasanians. Ancient Persia.*" http://www.livius.org/sao-sd/sassanids/sassanids.htm
16. Mādūn, Muḥammad ʿAlī. *Khaṭṭ al-Jazm ibn al-Khaṭṭ al-Musnad.* al-Ṭabʿah al-ʾŪlá. Dimashq: Dār Ṭlās lil-Dirāsāt wa-al-Terjamah wa-al-Nashr, 1989.
17. al-Maghribī, ʿIyāḍ bin Mūsá al-Yaḥṣibī al-Sabtī. *al-Sīrah al-Nabawiyyah: Kitāb al-Shafāʾ bi-Taʿrīf Ḥuqūq al-Muṣṭafá.* Dār al-Fikr, 2002.
18. al-Maḥallī, Jalāl al-Dīn, and Jalal al-Dīn al-Sayyūṭī. *Tafsīr al-Jalālayn.* Bayrūt: al-Ṭabʿah al-Thālithah. Dār al-Maʿrifah, 1984.
19. Makhlūf, Ḥusayn Muḥammad. *Ṣafwat al-Bayān li-Maʾānī al-Qurʾān.* al-Kūwayt: Wizārat al-Awqāf wa-al-Shu'ūn al-Islāmiyah, 1987. al-Ṭabʿah al-Thālithah.

20. al-Maʿrifah: al-Mawsūʾah al-Ḥurrah li-Khalq wa-Jamʿ al-Muḥtawá al-ʿArabī. *Mamlakat Tannūkh.* http://www.marefa.org
21. al-Marīkhī, Mishliḥ bin Kamīkh, Ghubān, ʿAlī Ibrāhīm. "*Naqsh Wāʾil bin al-Jazzāz al-Tidhkārī al-Muʾarrakh ʿām 410 Mīlādī.*" Silsilat Mudāwalāt al-Liqāʾ al-Sanawī lil-Jamʿiyyah 3. Masqaṭ, Jāmiʿat al-Sulṭān Qābūs, 2001.
22. al-Munjid al-Abjadī. al-Ṭabʿah al-Ūlá. Bayrūt: Dār al-Mashriq, 1967.
23. O'Connor, M. "The Arabic Loanwords in Nabataean Aramaic." *Journal of Near Eastern Studies.* 45, no. 3 (July 1986): 213-229
24. Patrich, Joseph. *The Formation of Nabataean Art: Prohibition of a Graven Image among the Nabataeans.* Jerusalem: The Magnes press.
25. Rabin, Chaim. *Ancient West Arabian.* London: Taylor's Foreign Press, 1951.
26. al-Ṣanʿānī, Muḥammad bin Ismaʿīl al-Amīr. *Subul al-Salām: Sharh Bulūgh al-Marām min Adillat al-Iḥkām.* Bayrūt: Dār al-Kutub al-ʿIlmiyyah, 2006.
27. Shahid, I. Philological Observations on Namara Inscription. *Journal of Semitic Studies.* 24 (1979): 33-42.
28. al-Ṭabarī, Abū Jaʿfar Muḥammad bin Jarīr. *Taʾrīkh al-Ṭibarī: Taʾrīkh al-Rusul wa-al-Mūlūk.* al-Qāhirah: Dār al-Maʿārif, 1977.
29. Wenning, Robert. "The Betyls of Petra." *Bulletin of the American Schools of Oriental Research* 324 (November 2001): 79-95.
30. Wikībīdyah: al-Mawsūʿah al-Ḥurrah. "al-Manādhirah." http://ar.wikipedia.org

31. Winnett, F. V. "A Himyaritic Inscription from the Persian Gulf Region." *Bulletin of the American Schools of Oriental Research.* 102 (April 1946): 4-6.
32. Wright, W. *A Grammar of the Arabic Language.* London: Cambridge University Press, 1955. Third Edition.

CHAPTER 4

The *Sa'adTa'lib* Musnad Arabic Inscription (~250 CE)

4.1 Introduction

Choosing a Musnad inscription from Yemen (or from anywhere else in the Arabian Peninsula) to support the research and main conclusions of this book is quite easy —there are more than 90,000 Musnad inscriptions found all over Arabia — from the farthest southern territory of Yemen to the farthest northern areas of the Fertile Crescent. Musnad, as we will discuss in Chapter 5, is the oldest known pre-Islamic Arabic script. The mere abundance and vast geographical coverage of these inscriptions is, by itself, an extremely valuable piece of information. It confirms that in those historical times, an overwhelming majority of the inhabitants of the Arabian Peninsula shared a uniform linguistic tool—the script. Emphatically, despite local dialectical variations, all Musnad inscriptions shared uniform and universal linguistic characteristics. It is most certain (or logical to hypothesize) that other minor tongues (with significantly different linguistic characteristics) that existed in the areas bordering with the core of old Arabia, had evolved with time into distinct languages. Decidedly though, they could not have been sister-languages — they were only derivative languages or even dialects.

To illustrate the common linguistic characteristics between classic Arabic and any old Arabic dialect, I decided to read a typical Musnad inscription from Yemen which is known for its distinct Arabic dialect. Reading a Musnad inscription from scratch, for the first time, I chose a never-read-before inscription to illustrate how easy can one with proper classic Arabic background read these inscriptions — more than eighty per cent of all available Musnad inscriptions are yet to be read. Dennis Carter, a retired American finance executive who lived for 53 years in the Arabian Gulf region, brought this inscription to my attention in August 2009. In 1967, Carter's father obtained the inscription, along with a few other alabaster heads and votive figures (see Figure 4.1), when he visited southern Arabia. He was told that the inscription stone (and the other pieces) were all found in the *Ma'rib* region of Yemen. For the purpose of this study, I named this inscription as the "*Sa'adTa'lib* Inscription," after the man who scribed it (or had it scribed). The inscription appears to belong to the period 250-300 CE, and it recorded the gold offering by *Sa'adTa'lib* to the south Arabian god *al-Miqh* (or *al-Maqah*) of the temple of *Awwm*, also known as *Maḥram Balqīs*, in *Ma'rib*.

To be accurate, I did not personally inspect the *Sa'adTa'lib* stone tablet. However, with Mr. Carter's help, I was able to obtain high quality photographs. According to his description, the well-preserved stone is of a light color, possibly granite; it weighs about 30 pounds, and is 12" high, 14" wide and about 2" deep. The overall quality of the inscription is good to excellent. It contained a total of eleven text lines in classic Sabaean Musnad script, all of which were written from right to left. The language of the inscription is — remarkably and clearly — Arabic. It included several solid usages of classic Arabic, flavored by local south Arabian dialect that is no more complex than my southern Iraqi Arabic dialect, as an example.

Figure (4.1) Alabaster head and votive figures from *Ma'rib*, Yemen. From the private family collection of Denise Carter, Santa Fe, New Mexico.

Reading my first Musnad inscription from scratch eliminated any remaining doubt that the old Yemeni language might not be Arabic. Not surprisingly, the only reference source I needed to read the inscription was the Arabic etymological dictionary: *Lisān al-ʿArab*, written by *Ibn Manẓūr* over one thousand years ago.[1]

The *Saʿad Taʾlib* inscription is a valuable comprehensive inscription, in that, it coherently illustrates several usages in the old Yemen's dialect, and sheds more light on the nature of the word *Sabaʾ* and a confusing period of Yemen's history.

4.2 Reading Musnad Inscriptions from Yemen

As with the language of similar old Yemenite inscriptions, reading the *Saʿad Taʾlib* inscription for the first time could induce one to believe that this language might not be Arabic. However, a more diligent examination would definitely reveal otherwise. To my surprise, reading this inscription was much easier than my first reading of a Nabataean Arabic inscription. This is because both grammar and vocabulary are clear and can be explained with classic Arabic tools. For example, the inscription used the definite article *al* four times for names and nicknames, which by itself is an overwhelming evidence of its "Arabicness." All what I needed to read the text successfully was to follow several observations and usages of a local dialect:

1. Written words are always spelled as pronounced in the dialect.

2. Each name mentioned in the inscription was followed immediately by either a nickname or a "wish verb," which seems to be a common old practice, as evidenced by numerous other Musnad inscriptions found in old Yemen.
3. The letter *mīm* at the end of a noun adds a factor of "greatness" or "plentiful" to it. This is referred to as *tamwīm* and has some of the effects of the classic Arabic *tanwīn,* but it is not a Yemenite replacement of it, as some believe. Using *mīm* to indicate greatness can even be seen in names used in other civilizations of the region, notably the Mesopotamian (Babylonian) mythological figure *Ut.napištu.m* (the Sumerian Noah's archetype who survived the flood in the Epic of Gilgamesh.)
4. The letter *nūn* at the end of a word is actually the letter *nūn* sound of Arabic *tanwīn*, not a Yemenite equivalent of the heavily used Arabic article *al* for 'the", as some scholars of Musnad believe today.
5. The letter combination *alif* and *lām* before a word is indeed the classic Arabic article *al* (the), which can be observed in several words in the current inscription.
6. The letter *hā'* at the beginning of a verb indicates the letter *alif* or *hamzah* forming the special case past tense verb as in *'a'ṭá* (gave) from *ya'ṭī* (to give).
7. The letter *hā'* at the end of a word could be the equivalent of classic Arabic usage of *tā' marbūṭah.*
8. The letter *dhāl* in the beginning of a noun or a verb could indicate *alladhī, dhī, dhā, dhū* الذي، ذي، ذا، ذو.

9. Vertical slashes indicate words' separations.

To our luck, the *Sa'adTa'lib* inscription uses all of the above listed observations.

4.3 Reading the *Sa'adTa'lib* Musnad Arabic Inscription

To illustrate the details of my reading, I provided an Arabic line-by-line, letter-by-letter transcription of the Musnad text of the inscription along with modern Arabic translation, Figure 4.2. Incidentally, I found no critical need to provide an image of my tracing since the picture is remarkably clear. Missing letters, which I could not confirm physically, are added between square brackets. Note: I will only discuss selective words in my reading, since the majority of words in this inscription are self-explanatory to anyone familiar with classic Arabic.

Line 1

The first word *Sa'adTa'lib,* or *Sa'dTa'lib* (pronounced *Sa'duTa'lib*) is the compound name of the person who initiated this inscription and presented the gift to the god of the temple. The first part of the name *Sa'd* or *Sa'ad* is a very common Arabic name meaning "happiness," which is often combined with a second noun in the meaning of "joy of" as in *Sa'du-al-Dīn* for "joy of the religion." The name *Sa'adTa'lib* means "joy of *Ta'lib*", where *Ta'lib* is either a name of a tribe or one of Yemen's gods. It should be noted, the combined name

Sa'dTa'lib seems to be a common name at that time, since it had appeared in several other Musnad inscriptions and is believed to be the name of the top military leader of the most famous king of Yemen, *Shimr Yar'ish*, who ruled, according to most accounts, c. 250-300 CE.

The following word *Yaqliṭ* is a verb used as a "wish or desire" verb for that person; it should not be confused with a standard nickname, which is usually an adjective or a noun. Using verbs in such a manner is a common old southern Arab-

Figure (4.2) The *Sa'adTa'lib* inscription stone (~ 250 CE), *Ma'rib*, Yemen. From the private family collection of Denise Carter, Santa Fe, New Mexico, USA.

Isolated letter-by-letter Arabic transcription from the *Musnad* script

سعدتألب | يقلط | بن | عثكلن | عصيت | و[بنا]

عم | وأخيهو | ألوهب | أصحح | ورثدم | يغن

م | موضعم | هقنيو | ألمقه | ثهون | بعل | أوم | صلمنه |

ذهبن | لوفي | مرأيهمو | ألشرح | يحضب | وأخيهو | [ي]

[أ]زل | بين | ملكي | سبأ/ظفر| وذريدن | بني | فرعم | ينهب [ا]

عك | سبأ | ولوفي | عبدهمي | سعدتألب | بن | عثكلن |

موضعم | وأخيهو | ألوهب | ورثدم | بني | موضعم | و[ل]

ورثدم | بذت | هوفي | ألمقه | عبدهو | سعدتألب | ب[نا]

أملص | سيملأ | بعمهو | حمدمل | ذت | خير | وهوف[ي] |

ألمقه | عبدهو | سعدتألب | بن | مرض | وحلي | عن

هم | ذظفهو | بيوم | ثلثمأه | ...

Modern Arabic equivalence

سَعْدْ تألب، يَقلِط، بن عثكلان، عَصَيْتَ، وبن عمو أخيهُ الوهاب، الصُحاح، ورثدم، يَغنمْ، مُوضِعُ ، أقنيو المقهْ، ثُهون، بَعْلُ أوْمْ، صَلْمَنَةِ ذَهَبٍ، لوفي سيديهمُ الشرح، يَحضِب، وأخيه يأزل، بيِّنْ، ملكيّ سبأ وذي ريدِن، بنو فارعٍ، يَنْهِب، عَكْ سَبَأ، ولوفي عَبداهما سَعْدْ تألب بن عثكلان مُوضِعُ واخيهُ الوهاب ورثدم، بنو مُوضِعٍ، ولوَفي ورثدم بذاتهِ. أوفى المقهْ عَبْدَهُ سَعْدْ تألب من إمْلاص، سيَعيش بفضل عمّه، حمداً له، ذات خير. وأوفى المقهْ عَبْدَهُ سَعْدْ تألب من مَرضٍ وحِلي. عَنْهُمُ الذي اضافهُ بيومٍ ثلاثِمئة ..

Figure (4.3) The *Sa'adTa'lib* inscription (~ 250 CE), *Ma'rib*, Yemen, with a line-by-line, letter-by-letter, transcription from *Musnad* and translation into modern Arabic by the author.

ian practice seen in most Musnad inscriptions. As tradition had it, following a name with a "wishing verb" that is in the past tense when a person is dead, and in the present tense when the person is alive, was a common Arabian practice that survived till present time. After Islam, many "wish verbs" were linked to god as in *raẓiyah Allāh 'anh* رضي الله عنه (may God be pleased with or accept him), *waffaqahū Allāh* وفقه الله (may God make him successful), *yaḥfuẓuhu Allā* يحفظه الله (may God protect him), and many more. It seems that in southern Arabia, these "wish verbs" were more personalized, but some of them were reserved for a shared figure, too. A good example for reserving a "wish verb" to an important figure is Islamic use of the phrase *ṣallá Allāh 'alayhi wa-sallam* صلى الله عليه وسلم (God prayed for him and saluted him,) each time the prophet Muhammad is mentioned. The present tense verb *Yaqliṭ* used in the *Sa'adTa'lib* inscription, means "move ahead" or "move on." This verb is still being used today in many Arabian regions, including southern Iraq.

The word *bin* after *Yaqliṭ* means "son of" but it can also be used as *min* (from), clearly a matching usage since a son is "from" his father. The word *'thkln*, which is likely *'Athkalān* (a well-known name of a contemporary tribe in Yemen) is actually the first name of his father. It was followed by the word *'ṣyt*, which is possibly *'aṣayta,* past tense of *ya'ṣī* (to resist). A past tense verb was used in this case, maybe because it was assigned to him after he died.

Line 2

The phrase *bin ʿam waʾakhīhū* could mean "his cousin and stepbrother;" however, since there was no letter *wāw* or *hāʾ* after the *mīm* in *ʿam*, I firmly believe the *wāw* of *waʿakhīhu* is referring or related to the first word *ʿam* (uncle), thus turning the phrase into *bin ʿammū akhīhū*, which literally means "his cousin, his brother." The word *ʿam* does not fit here by itself without an attached referral article. This argument is similar to my early argument on the topic of the introductory phrase — *nafs wa-qabr* — found in most eastern Arabian tombs, which according to my research should be pronounced *nafsū qabr*. Recall, in Chapter 3.3, the usage in the *Umm al-Jimāl* Arabic Nabatatean inscription of this phrase as *nafsū qabr* in the meaning of *huwa nafsuhū qabr*.

Very likely, the word *ʾlwhb* is the name of *Saʾd Taʾlib* cousin. It is possibly either *al-Wahb* or *al-Wahhāb* as in the common Arabic first names *Wahb* or *Wahhāb*. In such case, the addition of *al* in the beginning, is for extra recognition or acknowledgment, another common classic Arabic practice. The word *ʾṣḥḥ* is likely his nickname. This word could be starting with *alif-hamzah* or the Arabic article *al* but with the letter *lām* removed since it is not pronounced, as in the case of *al-Wahb*. In the first case it would be a wish verb in the meaning of *aṣḥiḥ or ṣaḥḥiḥ*, as in "make correct." In the second and more likely case, the word could be *al-Ṣaḥḥāḥ* to mean "the corrector" or "the justice maker." Another possibility for the second case is that this word stands for al-*Ṣiḥḥiḥ, al-Ṣiḥḥāḥ*, or even *al-Ṣaḥḥāḥ,* in relation to the Arabic verbs ṣiḥ or *aṣḥiḥ* from *ṣiḥḥah* which means "health." Therefore, it would mean "the healer," which is possibly his profession. The next word is *al-Wahb's* father name, *Wirthdam,* as in *Wirth al-Damm.* Alternatively, it could be another name with the added *mīm* for "greatness." The wish verb following his cousin and stepbrother's father name, *yaghnim,* is a present tense verb in the meaning of "wish he becomes more prosperous." Using a present tense indicates he is still alive.

Line 3

The first two words are traced as *Mwdh'm haqnayū.* The grandfather's name *Mwdh'm* is possibly *Mūdhi'* with the final *mīm* added for "greatness." The word *haqnayū* is *aqnayū* which is derived from *aqnā* أقنا for "gave forever."

The next phrase is traced as *'lmqh thhwn ba'l 'wm* and is referring to their god. The first word *'lmqh* is claimed by some scholars to be derived from *īl* (supposedly the word god in Hebrew) and *maqah* (protecting.) I found no evidence supporting this reading. *Ibn Manẓūr* indicated in *Lisān al-'Arab* that the root word مقه (no diacritics were added) has plenty of meanings, including "shining white." According to his book, *al-maqh* (could also be *al-miqh*) and *al-amqah* are all adjectives in the meaning of "the shining white." It follows clearly, in this inscription, as in the numerous other Musnad inscriptions of Yemen, this word is *al-Maqh* or *al-Miqh,* using the Arabic article *al* (not Hebrew *īl,)* which is the name of the god in the meaning of *al-nāṣi' al-bayāḍ* الناصع البياض (the shining white) or *al-nūr* (the light.) *Ibn Manẓūr* also listed the following Islamic *Ḥadīth* المقة من الله والصيت من السماء in which the word *al-Maqh* means "love". It is also possible, that the word *al-Miqh* is referring literally to the shining "moon god," as it is believed and indicated by most sources. However, based on the rest of the inscription, it can be a name of a golden statue, too. The meaning of *al-Maqh,* which conveys the image of bright light, fits the description of a shining golden statue, as well as a bright white moon, which is the exact given meaning of the word *miqh* by *Lisān al-ʿArab.*

The following word is likely *thuhūn* ثُهون or *thuhuna* ثُهُن, but it can also be *thahwān* ثهوان , or *thāhūn* ثاهون , all of which are related to the verb *thahata* ثَهَتَ or *thahana* ثَهَنَ (to pray, or call upon someone for help while crying with tears). The word is therefore a verb or verb-like title for the god *al-Miqh* in the meaning of *ikhshaʿū lahu* اخشعو له, *al-khushūʿ lahu* الخشوع له, *idʿū lahu* ادعو له, *al-duʿā' lah* الدعاء له (the one to pray to, or who is prayed to.) The practice of adding a verb after the name of a god is universal among the Arabs. Even after Islam, they used the verb *taʿālá* تعالى after *'Allāh* (God.) Some believe *thuhūn* is a separate name, although based on the usage described in this inscription, yet, such possibility is highly unlikely. It is possible though that this word was used alone (without *al-Miqh*) to refer to him, just as we say today *qala taʿālá* (God said) instead of *qāla Allāh taʿālá.*

In the next phrase *baʿl ʾwm*, the word *baʿl* could either mean *sanam* (statue of an idol) or *rab* / *ʾIlāh* (god of). In the Quran (37:125), we read the following verse أَتَدْعُونَ بَعْلًا وَتَذَرُونَ أَحْسَنَ الْخَالِقِينَ (why do you pray to *a statue* and forget about the perfect God,) which clearly uses the word *baʾl* as either "a statue" or a name of a statue. *Lisān al-ʿArab* explains that the word *baʿl* could mean "god" or "owner"; but it could have also been the name of a golden idol statue worshiped by the Arabs before Islam.

The word after *baʿl* is traced as *ʾAwwm*, as it did not include the *al* article. This word is most likely the name of the temple where the golden statue of the god *al-Miqh* is placed. The Arabic word *aww* (sheltering or shelter) can be a noun of the verbs *awā* or *awá* (sheltered) according to *Lisān al-ʿArab*. Likely, the final *mīm* is added to make it sound as a "grand shelter." Alternatively, the word can be a name, *Awwām* (the place giving shelter,) but this is less likely because in standard Arabic the name should then be *awwāʾ*, as in *rawá* and *rawwāʾ*. The phrase *Baʿl ʾAwwām* can therefore be "statue or idol of *Awwm*", "*Baʿl* of *Awwm*", or "god of *Awwm*" (the temple of *Maʾrib*.)

The first word, *ṣlmnh*, of the next two-word phrase is derived from *ṣalam,* which was used throughout Arabia for a special type of *ṣanam* (statue of an idol). *Lisān al-ʿArab* indicates that the word *ṣalam* was used to decribe someone (including an idol statue), whose ears were either cut off or it was simply earless — which is the case with most alabaster heads and votive figures found in *Ma'rib* and elsewhere (see Figure 4.1.) *Lisān al-'Arab* also indicates that this word could be used as the verb *iqtaṭa'a* (cut from,) or the noun *qaṭ'* (piece of.) Adding the *nūn* and *ha'* at the end would make it *qiṭ'ah* قطعة, a feminine noun—that is how I read the word as *ṣalamanah* or *ṣalmanah.* Interestingly, the Hebrew Bible uses this word as the name of the geographical location, where according to the Jewish religion, Moses led his followers after speaking with God in Mount Sinai.

Line 4

The word *dhahabun* is *dhahab* ذهبٌ with Arabic *tanwīn.* Together with the previous word, the phrase becomes *ṣalamanah dhahbun* for either "an earless female statue made of gold," or "a piece of gold." The word *lwfī* is *li-wafyī* لوفَي instead, means *li-ḥifẓ* لحفظ ("to keep" or "to protect".) This word is related to the noun *wafā'.* The word *mar'ayhumu* is derived from *mar'* or *'umru'* (person). This word was used here in the meaning of "master." You may recall the name of the most important pre-Islamic king *Ūmru' al-Qays.* Based on classic Arabic grammar, adding the letter *yā'* after a noun as in *mar'ayhumu* indicates that they were two masters. The name of the first king was *al-Shirḥ* followed by the "wish verb" *Yaḥdhib*, possibly in the meaning of "wish he will ignite more fire." Some referred to him as *'il Sharah*, possibly hinting at the Hebrew use of *'il* for god. Again, this is very unlikely since the word *al-Shirh* appears as one word, clearly indicating that *al* is the Arabic article "the"— added for extra respect.

Line 5

The second king's name is *Y'zil* followed by the word *bayyin*, this verb maybe derived from *yubayyin,* which could mean "differentiate between" or "to clarify." It may also be the adjective *bayyin* (clear.) The word that follows, *malikay,* is from *malik* (king.) It means "the two kings of;" this is another classic Arabic usage. The name *Saba'* is for the city or the tribe of *Saba'*. Originally, Saba' was likely the name of a tribe founder, but afterwards became a name of a tribe, and eventually the name of the city/state kingdom of *Saba'* in southeastern Yemen. The ensuing name *Dhrīdn* ذريدن is actually *Dhī Rīdin* ذي ريدن. As mentioned earlier, the letter *dhāl* in the beginning of a noun is for *dhū*, *dhī*, or *alladhī.* This word means the people of *Rīdan*, a city (or the location or estate of tribe) near *Ma'rib*, which was conquered by the Kingdom of *Saba'* and became the capital around a century later. The phrase, therefore, could be read as "the two kings of *Saba'* and *Dhī Rīdan.*"

In examining the traced word *Saba'* in this line, one could also trace another word placed over it. It seems that, at one point in time, someone tried to erase the word *Saba'* to replace it with the word *ẓfr.* Convincingly, this could be the ancient city *Ẓafar* ظفار that was later replaced by the nearby city of *Ṣan'ā'* as the new capital of the Himyarite Kingdom of northern Yemen. In turn, this suggests that the Himyarite

Kingdom was close to capturing the *Saba'* Kingdom in that period thus required scribes to change the kingdom name from "*Saba'* and *Dhī Rīdan,*" southeastern of Yemen today, to "*Ẓafar* and *Dhī Rīdan,*" which, not incidentally, are all situated in modern Yemen.

Alternatively, but more likely, the word *ẓfr* could be *Ẓifār* (*Ḥaḍramawt*), modern Oman. This may suggest that the kingdom of *Saba'* was taken over by *Ẓifār* under the rule of the two brother kings and renamed their kingdom, *Ẓifar* and *Dhī Rīdan.* Since most historians consider the Himyarite king, *Shimr Yarʿish,* as the first king to unify all of Yemen, including *Ẓifār* (c. 300 CE,) and that the two southern Yemenite kings cited in this inscription had ruled directly before (or directly after) him. Consequently, it is my conviction that this inscription should be dated c. 250-300 CE. Regrettably, the final line that most likely listed the exact date was partially damaged.

As for the name of the father of the two kings, it was either *Firʿ* or *Fāriʿ* and was followed by the letter *mīm* for greatness. The "wish verb" after it, *Yanhib*, means, "Wish he get more war lootings." Surprisingly, on the next line, the first word was not *malk*, but clearly *ʿAk,* a known Arabic first name, which could be the kings' grandfather's name. As we have seen earlier, the inscription has already listed, in two other lines, a name of a grandfather: *Mūdhiʿ*, without using the usual Arabic *bin* (son of.) Alternatively, *ʿAk* could be a title of some sort. The next word, *Saba'*, is either their great grandfather's name or a nickname turned into a tribe name, not necessarily a city name. This fact would confirm Muslim historians' classification of the word. In the Quran, for example, the word *Saba'* appeares twice. The first in *Sūrat al-Naml* (27:21) وجِئْتُكَ مِن سَبَإٍ بِنَبَإٍ يَقِينٍ. إِنِّي وَجَدتُّ امْرَأَةً تَمْلِكُهُمْ. The second in *Sūrat Saba'* (34:15) لَقَدْ كَانَ لِسَبَإٍ فِي مَسْكَنِهِمْ آيَةٌ. Both references use the word in the meaning of *banī Saba'* (tribe of *Saba'*) similar to *banī 'Asad*, for example.

Line 6

The word *wlwfī* is *wa-li-wafyī*, or *wa-li-ḥifẓi* (and to protect.) The following word *'bdhmy* is likely *'abdahumá* عبداهمى in the meaning of *'abdahumā* عبداهما referring to *Sa'dTa'lib* alone, as the slave of both kings; but it can also be *'abdāhumā*, referring to both, *Sa'dTa'lib* and his cousin *al-Wahhāb*.

Line 8

The word *bdht* means *bi-dhāta* بذاتَ or *bi-dhātih* بذاته (himself) referring to his uncle *Wirthdam*. Therefore, the entire phrase *wa-li-Wirthdam bi-dhāta*, extending from the previous line, means *wa-li-hifẓ Wirthdam bi-dhātih.* The word *hwfī* is *'awfá,* replaces *alif* with *hā',* which means *ḥafaẓa*. Even today, starting a sentence with a past tense verb is a standard Arabic practice in religious statements as in "*ḥafaẓa Allāh Fulān.*"

Line 10

The word *'mlṣ* is most definitely *imlāṣ* إملاص which, according to *Lisān al-'Arab*, means *inzilāq* انزلاق (slipping,) or *infilāt*, which probably means in this context: "falling to temptations", or "wrong doing". The previous word, at the end of the line above, shows the letter *bā'* on its own. I tend to think though that this letter must have been followed by a partially damaged letter *nūn* to make up the word *bin* in the meaning of "from". The word *sayamla'* سيملئ literally means "Will be filled up or completed." Again, my opinion is that it means "will be raised appropriately" since the following word was *bi-'ammahū* بعمه as in *bi-faẓl 'ammahu* بفضل عمه (by his uncle's kindness.) This, necessarily, confirms that *Sa'dTa'lib*'s father was dead.

The word *ḥmdml* is an interesting word as it appears in many other Sabaean *Musnad* inscriptions. It seems like a commonly used abbreviated vernacular phrase, in the meaning of present-day Arabic phrase "*hamdan lah,*" "*ḥamdan lillāh,*" or "*al-ḥamdu lillāh.*" I believe the letter *mīm* of *ḥamdam* (thanks to) is not Arabic *tanwīn* but Arabic *tamwīm* in the meaning of "*ḥamdan kabīr*" or "*ḥamdan 'adhīm*" (many thanks to.) The following phrase *dht khyr* is *dhāt khayr* as in "generous one with good deed" or possibly "one who is well to do." The word *ḥlī* or *ḥalī* takes the meaning of "dryness" among others. Possibly, it is used here in the meaning of "poverty" or "need".

Line 11

This line is, evidently, the final line of the inscription since it is stating the inscription date and the person adding it to the temple. Sadly, it is badly damaged; hence, I was only able to read it partially. The first word, extending from the previous line, is *ʿanhum* عنهم as in *bil-niyābati ʿanhum* بالنيابة عنهم (for them.) It was followed by the word *dhẓfhw* for *dhū ẓāfahū* ذو ضافهو or *alladhi ẓāfahū* الذي اضافه (he who added it,) possibly referring to *Sa'dTa'lib* and the piece of gold, or earless golden statue, or the inscription record itself. The final but partially legible word of the inscription was possibly *thlthm'h* for *thulthumā'ah* ثلثمائة (three hundreds.) Its final *hā'* is the same as *tā' marbūṭah.*

4.4 Conclusion

Reading this inscription, one can see without any doubt, the extent of classic (or standard) Arabic language used throughout the words of the inscription! According to my detailed reading above, I can summarize the detailed English translation with appropriate explanation as follows:

> *SaʿadTa'lib* (name of the presenter), *Yaqliṭ* (meaning "to advance") son of *ʿAthkalān* (his father's name) *ʿAṣayta* (meaning "did not succumb") and his cousin, (possibly and) his brother, *al-Wahhāb* (his name) *al-Suḥāḥ* (nickname meaning "the correct") *Wirthdam* (his father's name who is *SaʿadTa'lib* uncle and possibly stepfather) *Mūḍiʿim* (*Mūḍiʿ,* their grandfather's name) *Yaghnim* (meaning "to prosper") offered *al-Maqh* (name of the god meaning "the shining light") *thuhūn* (meaning "pray to him" or "the one prayed to"), golden statue of *'Awwm* temple, a piece (or earless statue) of gold, to protect their

two masters, *al-Shirḥ* (his name) *Yaḥḍib* (meaning "to ignite") and his brother *Yi'zil* (his name) *Bayyin* (meaning "to clarify or differentiate"), the two kings of *Saba'* (city or tribe) and *Dhī* (people of) *Raydin* (city or tribe), sons of *Fāri'im* (*Fāri'*, their father's name) *Yanhib* (meaning "to take over") *'Ak* (their grandfather's name) *Saba'* (name of a person or possibly verb meaning "raided"), and to protect their two slaves *Sa'adTa'lib* son of *'Athkalān Mūḍi'im* and his brother *al-Wahhāb Wirthdam*, sons and grandsons of *Mūḍi'i*, and to protect *Wirthdam* himself. May *al-Maqh* protect his slave *Sa'adTa'lib* from wrongdoing, he will be raised by the kindness of his uncle who is, thanks to *al-Maqh* (the god), virtuous and prosperous, and may *al-Maqh* (the god), protect his slave *Sa'adTa'lib* from sickness and poverty. For them, he who added it (the gold or inscription) in the day three hundreds ......

The above English reading can be translated in Arabic, with explanation, as follows:

سعدتألب (اسم المتقدم)، يقلط (بمعنى ليتقدم)، بن عثكلن (عثكلان، اسم ابيه)، عَصَيْتَ (بمعنى عصى عليهم) وبن عم واخيهو (وبن عمو اخيه، او وبن عم واخيه، ربما هو اخيه من أمه ايضا) ألوهب (وهاب، اسمه) أصحح (بمعنى صحّحْ او الصحاح، لقبه) ورثدم (اسم ابيه وهو عم سعدتألب) يغنم (بمعنى ليغنم)، مُوضِعِم (موضعٌ، اسم جَديْهما او عشيرتهما)، هقنيو (أقْنَيو أو وهبو) ألمقه (المقه: اسم الاله بمعنى الناصع البياض)، ثُهون (بمعنى صلّي له)، بَعل (صنم

او إله) أوْم (معبد أوم او أوام)، صلمنه ذَهَبَن (قطعة او صنمة من ذهبٍ)، لوَفْيِ (لحفظ) مَرأيهمو (سيديهما) ألشرح (شرح، اسمه) يَحْضِب (بمعنى ليؤجج النار) واخيه يأزل (اسمه) بَيِّنْ (بمعنى وَضّح او ميّز)، ملكيّ سبأ (اسم مدينة او عشيرة) وذي (اهل، قوم) ريدن (اسم مدينة او عشيرة)، بني (ابناء واحفاد) فرعم (فارعٌ، اسم ابيهما) ينهب (بمعنى ليسلب) عَك (اسم جدهما) سبأ (اسم ابيه او ربما فعل بمعنى سبى)، ولوَفْي (ولحِفظ) عبدهمي (عبديهما) سعدتألب بن عثكلان مُوضِعِم واخيهُ إلوهاب ورثدم، بني (بنو أو أبناء) موضعم، ولورثدم (ولحفظ ورثدم) بذت (بذاته). هوفي (أوفى أو حَفَظَ) ألمقه (الإله المقه) عبده سعدتألب بن (من) إملص (إملاص اي انزلاق او عمل فاحش)، سيملئ (سيعيش برَغَد ويكتمل او يتربّى) بعمّه (بفضلِ عمه وربما زوج امه ايضا، ورثدم)، حمدمل (حمداً عظيماً له اي للإله المقه)، ذت خير (انه، اي ورثدم، ذات خير أي فاعل خير)، وهوفي (وحَفَظَ) ألمقه (الإله المقه) عَبده سعدتألب بن (من) مرض (مَرَضٍ) وحلي (وفاقة، عوز، أو فقر). عنهم (نيابةً عنهم) ذظفهو (الذي أضافه، ربما يقصد الذهب او النقش) بيوم ثلثمئه (ثلاثِ مئة ....

Bibliography

1. Ibn Manẓūr, Abū al-Faḍl Jamāl al-Dīn Muḥammad bin Mukarram. *Lisān al-ʿArab.* http://www.islamweb.net/newlibrary/

CHAPTER 5

Tracing the Arabic Script from Musnad to Jazm

5.1 Introduction

Studying the origins of the modern Arabic script is an important undertaking that goes beyond the mere history of the script. Yet, studying how Arabic evolved to its current forms is the first step to understand its past and secure its future; it is inspirational to know how the Arabic script performed its functions and how it interacted with its changing environments throughout history.

For many centuries, scholars of the past Islamic Arab civilization differed on the origin of the script. Their main differences centered though on what group of Arab tribes had used it first. But when the discovery of modern inscriptions hinted at possible Aramaic Nabataean or Syriac roots, this topic became highly complex, divisive, and charged, due to preconceived political beliefs on all sides. Strong indications confirm that current Western theories regarding the origin of the Arabic script are primarily governed by their eagerness to strip the Arabic script from its generating matrix to complement an overall, predetermined, de-Arabization theme. Said in other words, the intent seems to exclude, arbitrarily, any older Arabic Musnad roots by claiming with *uncompromised certainty* that modern Arabic was fully derived from one of the Aramaic scripts. Consequent to this, most modern-day books and articles discussing this subject just routinely restate the theories and conclusions made by the 19th century Western scholars after reading a handful of Nabataean inscriptions. They rehash the unsubstantiated notion positing that the Nabataean script had itself transformed into Arabic, without providing any convincing evidence or cogent debate. Some scholars, like *Muḥammad 'Alī Mādūn*, challenged this notion with serious analysis and methodical reasoning. He argued, while providing detailed illustrations, about a possible transformation mechanism of the older pre-Islamic Arabic Musnad shapes into their modern Arabic script ones. [18] Regrettably, books and articles written by other Arab scholars who disagree with the Aramaic Nabataean and Syriac origin theory, do not even attempt to offer any alternative convincing argument or analysis.

Discussing all early inscriptions and manuscripts with due attention given to details, is not my primary focus of this concise chapter. Instead, I am going to concentrate on a summary discussion of the most relevant inscriptions, papyri, and manuscripts available to us, and study the overall evidence presented in them within its proper geo-historical settings. My target is the pertinent examination of the important factors that shaped the early decades surrounding the birth of the modern Arabic script, Jazm. In this regard, speculating about the shapes of a letter in a few inscriptions is, to say the least, inadequate methodology to draw definite conclusions. Decidedly, studying the origins of the Arabic script must be carried out within the context of the scriptural, sociological, and geographical realities that were prevalent in the old Near East of that time.

5.2 Early Alphabets and the Emergence of Cursive Styles

According to modern day scholars, the earliest inscriptional evidence we have of an alphabet in the greater Arabian Peninsula, including the Fertile Crescent, was found in the eastern Mediterranean region located between ancient Mesopotamia (Iraq) and Egypt. It was dated back to the 14th century BCE. Collectively, the ancient shapes and forms of this alphabet are referred to as the Canaanite alphabet, which is commonly believed as the progenitor of most alphabets of the ancient world. [36] It is not clear why Western scholars have assumed that this alphabet had taken origins from a proto-Sinaic script that was *possibly* invented in Egypt, not the Levant itself or one of the population centers of the Arabian Peninsula, particularly Yemen, where most people of the Fertile Crescent had migrated from earlier. Comparing the primitive shapes of the so-called proto-Sainic alphabet found in a relatively few inscriptions in the Sinai desert, with those seen in the many thousands of inscriptions found in the adjacent vast Arabian Desert, one would conclude that these shapes actually belong to a single loosely-defined and concurrently-used ancient script. Since it is a fact that old cities of the Near East have used several, well-developed writing systems much earlier, why would they then need to adapt newer alphabets from the Sinai Desert, which is not known to have produced one single population center? The assumption of a Canaanite alphabet with a Sinai origin sounds more like a theory to confirm Biblical mythology than a scholarly theory. Surely, no one can prove that the few inscriptions found in the Sinai Desert are definitely much older than the ones found in the neighboring Arabian deserts, especially since the two contained, more or less, identical and primitive shapes.

Casting more doubts over this proto-Sinaic origin theory, archeologists have also uncovered evidence for the existence of another old alphabetic writing system in the same geographical area and during the same time period of the Canaanite Alphabet; that is the Ugaritic alphabet of the city-state of Ugarit, near *Rās Shamrah* in northern Syria. The Ugaritic script had two alphabet styles: long one with 30 letters, and short one with 22 letters. All Ugaritic letters had Mesopotamian Cuneiform shapes with text written left to right. It is not fully clear whether Ugaritic was a special adaptation of an Egyptian-related Canaanite alphabet, or an earlier alphabet of Mesopotamian origin.

It should be an accepted truth that inscriptions, alone, cannot provide, each time and always, indisputable evidence on the precise timelines of the birth of ancient scripts. Consequently, it is neither possible nor plausible that every time a newly found inscription becomes known, theorists would jump to give their final word as when a specific script had started. However, based on inscriptions of the ninth and early tenth centuries BCE, it is reasonable to state that two well-formed alphabets, containing many common shapes and sharing a similar overall look and feel, had existed in the greater Arabian Peninsula.

One was the Phoenician alphabet of the eastern Mediterranean, which scholars think was directly derived from the earlier Canaanite alphabet or even a transformed Canaanite. The second was the Arabic Musnad alphabet of the Arabian Peninsula including ancient Yemen, which most experts believe was a more developed kin of the parent Canaanite script, not Phoenician. Inscriptions further reveal that over a century later, another alphabet, Aramaic, clearly a variant of Phoenician, was used throughout the Fertile Crescent area and maybe Persia.

Some experts believe that the Phoenician script was actually derived from the Musnad Arabic script. German philologist and Indologist, Friedrich Max Müller (1823-1900) thought it was adapted from Musnad during the 9th century BCE, when the Minaean Kingdom of Yemen controlled areas of the eastern Mediterranean. The well-known Syrian scholar of the 19th century, *Shakīb 'Arsalān,* shares this view. [18]

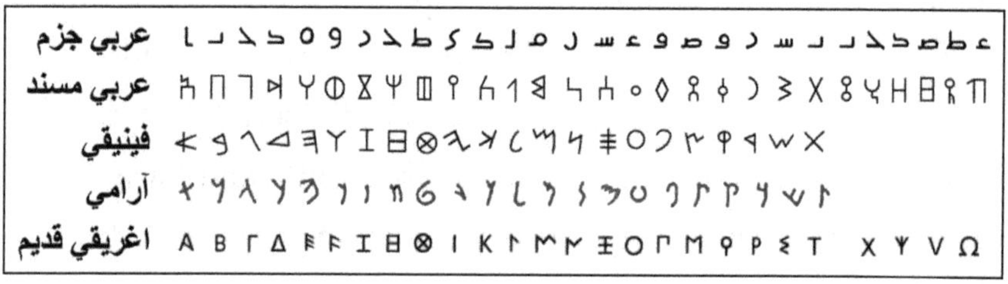

Figure (5.1) Table of rough shapes of a few early alphabets' characters.

Because of shape similarities between several Greek and Musnad letters, some experts believe that even Greek was derived directly from Musnad! After all, it is known that ancient Greece had extensive trade relations with Yemen, via the Red Sea, that went back to the 9th century BCE. Moreover, unlike Phoenician, which was exclusively right-to-left script, Musnad was bidirectional. This may explain the ancient Greek Boustrophedon practice of bidirectional writing.

Other scholars argued the opposite: that Musnad could have been adapted from the Phoenician script during the Minaean times. Nevertheless, the restricted ordering of characters in Phoenician makes this very unlikely. Still, regardless of their exact starting dates and origins, the undisputed archeological fact is that Musnad and Phoenician clearly share common roots and shapes and can equally be considered as the earliest developed and widely used alphabet of the Near East. Proving this point, the earliest found inscriptions of both scripts, with relatively well-defined shapes, belong, more or less, to the same time period, namely 9-10th century BCE.

Inscriptions found in the Near East, dating back to the third or fourth century BCE, showed that Aramaic and its derived scripts had eventually replaced Phoenician, thus becoming one of the major scripts of the Fertile Crescent. Inscriptions of that period also show that a semi-cursive script, sharing with Aramaic its 22 letters and most shapes, was widely used by several population centers in the southern areas of greater Syria and Iraq. This was the script of the ancient city of Petra, capital of the Nabataean kingdom, which was founded around the 3rd century BCE. The Nabataeans were predominantly Arab tribes settling in the area controlling trade routes from the eastern Mediterranean to *Ḥijāz* (Western Saudi Arabia) and Yemen. Based on comparative research, the Nabataeans appear to have adapted a script with slightly modified Aramaic shapes consequent to centuries of trade relations with neighboring urban centers.

Most scholars believe that the Nabataean script was derived from the Syriac script around the 2nd century BCE. However, they offer no convincing evidence to support such claim. While the earliest Nabataean inscriptions on the walls of

Figure (5.2) One of many Nabataean inscriptions that can be seen today on the walls of Petra. [32]

Figure (5.3) The Tripod Mosaic Syriac inscription, Urfa, Turkey. Dated 3rd century CE. [30]

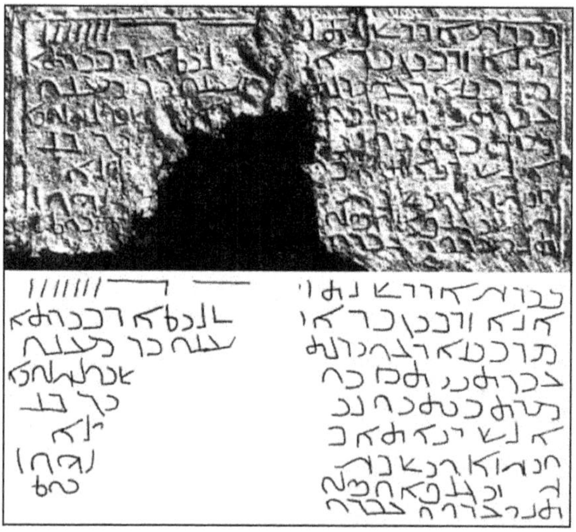

Figure (5.4) Earliest found Syriac inscription dated 6 CE. [12]

ancient Petra date back to the 3rd century BCE, the earliest found inscriptions of the Syriac script are from the 1st century CE. Syriac, like Nabataean is clearly derived from or related to Aramaic. According to found inscriptions, Syriac was first used in Odessa, currently Urfa in southern Turkey. [12]

By the 3rd or 4th century BCE, the practice — so it seems — of connecting letter shapes had become popular in the greater Arabian Peninsula and Persia. This trend was most likely the result of the introduction of newer inscription media and tools, thus making letter connectivity a marker for a new era in script development, as it transformed ancient scripts in the same way complete detachment transformed modern scripts in the age of typography. Cursive writing necessitated radical changes to the shapes of letters. Letters were flipped, rotated, extended, or completely replaced to adhere to the new cursive rules. The new words absorbed the actual, visual characteristics of individual letters. Scripts that traditionally utilized open order, like Musnad, assumed one direction in cursive styles. [27] Within this new cursive environment, scripts adjusted differently. Some, like the Nabataean script, adapted full connectivity but kept most of its letters' shapes unaltered, while others changed shapes radically for the sake of connectivity. Examples include the cursive Musnad in Yemen, and maybe the Pahlavi of Persia. Other scripts, like Hebrew, ignored this new trend altogether. [2] The dynamics of script evolution, in that period, was a classical case illustrating how new forms dialectically emerge from the old ones.

By its evolutionary nature, the development of any script is not a linear process with precise connotations. Because of this nonlinearity and manifest uncertainty, a scientific research dealing with scripts' origins should include not only investigation, but also coherent speculation, reasoned interpretation, and probabilistic determinism. The conclusions presented in this study rest on a theoretical foundation: early forms of scripts rarely, maybe never, developed in an isolated environment or by decree. Instead, they evolved through adaptation to scripts of adjacent areas and to socioeconomic, materialistic needs. *Under normal circumstances, people do not abandon their writing systems abruptly in favor of another.*

Before embarking on the investigation of any script origin, one should first establish what a derived script is. Identification should take into account, the number of letters used, their visual characteristics, and the overall script dynamics. Comparing a small number of letter shapes alone is not enough to identify the origin of a script. Similarly, realizing cursive trends in an older inscription belonging to one script does not prove that a newer cursive script was necessarily derived from it. As we already stated, the study of a script development must be carried out within its sociological and geographical environments. Of a special note, a new script can be derived from multiple scripts' sources and not just a specific source. Most remarkable, a script can also be invented from scratch.

5.3 Birth of Jazm Script: Pre-Islamic Arabia and its Scripts

In the early centuries of the first millennium, the northern area of the greater Arabian Peninsula was a land of several old and new religions. Babylonia, once the undisputed cultural center in the region, was under the Persian Sassanid rule while the eastern Mediterranean coast was controlled by the Romans. In contrast, the middle and south regions of Arabia enjoyed a more homogeneous religious environment. They were free of direct foreign dominance. Still, despite sporadic presence of ancient Hebrews, Christians, and Mandaeans in the northern urban centers, the majority of the inhabitants of the Greater Arabian Peninsula, including the Fertile Crescent, were pagans. Like the people of Persia, they did not fully embrace monotheism until after the emergence of Islam.

Arab population centers and tribes roaming the heartland were not isolated from the religiously turbulent north. Traditionally, Arab tribes enjoyed strong ties with each other no matter where they settled. Historically, these tribes roamed large areas extending from Yemen to the upper Tigris and Euphrates. It is expected that in the course of their continuing movement, they had not only connected with various civilizations in the region, but also created new urban centers of their own. Many had settled throughout the Fertile Crescent long centuries before the Christian era, bringing along their gods, language, and script — the Musnad. The migration north continued unabated for centuries, even after Islam. In fact, Arabic-speaking Muslim armies moving north during the 7th century were at home in most population centers of Iraq and greater Syria. There is no single evidence that they used translators to communicate with local populations. History teaches us that before the emergence of Islam, Prophet Muhammad did not only trade goods, during his frequent visits to the Damascus area, but had also conversed about deep philosophical, sociological, and religious topics with local prominent figures in that area. Yet, he is known to speak one language: Arabic. It is true that before Islam, the Aramaic and Syriac languages were fully established in many areas of the Fertile Crescent, but so was the Nabataean Arabic, the language of the majority in the region, and old Arabic, their mother and matrix tongue.

Just before Islam, the local Aramaic scripts of the Fertile Crescent, like the Aramaic Language itself and its closely related dialects, had limited applications, as they were primarily religious, scripts. The dominant day-to-day scripts for business and government were those of the occupying neighboring powers, namely the Persians and Romans. During that period, local religions differentiated their written teachings from each other by creating exclusively derived religious scripts. Mandaeans, Manicheans, Christians, Zarothostians and Jews all had their religious scripts. Under external forces, the Fertile Crescent region was no longer a central player internationally or on a regional level. These foreign forces dominated the area militarily, culturally and economically. For the Arabs, however, one positive aspect emanated from that situation: the cultural treasures of the Persian and Roman civilizations were now within the direct reach of Arabia's heartland.

The development of the new Jazm Arabic script, probably in the early centuries of the Christian era, according to available inscriptions, should be studied within this diverse mosaic of cultures. Scripts with visually sophisticated curves like Pahlavi and Avesta were now used in nearby Mesopotamia. [23] Greek and Aramaic scripts as well as Nabataean, Syriac, and Mandaean were just north of *Ḥijāz*. Although the original Musnad Arabic script, in its varied styles, continued to be the main script of the Arabian Peninsula, it gradually lost its dominance in the north, since it became one among many scripts. Within this pluralistic environment, the young Arabic script must have been shaped, necessarily, by more than one script style.

The earliest style of the modern Arabic script was inspired and shaped by the more-developed surrounding scripts, the same way other newer and re-reinvented (recycled) scripts of the Near East were inspired and shaped by the Arabic-dominated environment after Islam. Older writing systems, particularly the Aramaic-derived religious ones, did not simply vanish. Despite their diminished use, they survived and even improved by adapting to the dominating Arabic script. Therefore, scholars should not view the present, post-Islamic, shapes of the surviving non-Arabic scripts of the Near East completely outside the frames of the Arabic script. Simply, it is unconceivable, even farfetched, to think that the surviving Aramaic scripts were immune to the overwhelming Arabic script environment after the advent of Islam.

Opting to discard this plain truth, some scholars embrace the opposite belief — that early Arabic was derived from Syriac or one of the other Aramaic scripts of the early centuries, like Mandaic, Manichean, or Palmyrene. However, inscriptions in that period revealed that Syriac, like early Nabataean, did not have any fully cursive style, predating Jazm. As we will discuss later, a trilingual inscription from the heartland of the Syriac script, Zabad, dated back to 512 CE, showed mostly isolated Syriac letterforms, side by side Greek and fully cursive Arabic texts. Early Syriac inscriptions showed no signs of diacritic marks or dots, either. In my view, the Arabic-like cursive and doted Syriac Estrangelo script of the Peshitta manuscripts, presented by some scholars today as from the 5th century CE, are from post-Islamic times, possibly the 12th century CE. That being said, from an evolutionary perspective, the Syriac script variants should still be thought of as authentic relatives of the modern Arabic script.

The above argument is also valid in relation to claims positing that early Arabic may have been derived from one of the highly artistic Persian scripts used in Mesopotamia during centuries of Sassanid rule. One cannot deny that the leap of Arabic to its magnificent shapes, during the Abbasid Caliphate, has Persian artistic imprints all over it. This is expected since Iraq (the melting pot center of the Abbasids Arabs) was under direct Persian rule from the 3rd century BCE until the

8th century CE, and had continued its heavy association with the Persian culture after Islam.

Figure (5.5) Pre-Islamic trilingual inscription of Zabad found near Aleppo, Syria, including Syriac (top left), Greek (top right) and Arabic (bottom) scripts dated 512 CE. [28] Arabic text is traced for clarity in the bottom.

However, the evolution of Jazm Arabic should not be confused with its origin. Pahlavi and Avesta inscriptions of the early centuries of the modern era show sophisticated curves, seamlessness, and rhythm that may have influenced the development of early Arabic letterforms. Then again, while both scripts showed more tendencies to connect letterforms than early Syriac, their connectivity was, nevertheless, reluctant and they did not share with the newly developing Jazm its major defining dynamics. In the 10th century, *Ibn al-Nadīm* described several old and new Persian scripts. *Al-Nadīm*'s sketches of some of the survived letters' shapes did not reproduce their original forms. Most sketches showed curves resembling those of old Pahlavi but not similar to those of Persian *Nasta'līq* style. Referring to an earlier version of one such script, he called *Firamūz* (sometimes cited as the Arabic-like

Persian script predating Arabic,) *Ibn al-Nadīm* explained, "It was derived from and wrote by the Persians. It is a recent development in two forms." His statement clearly indicates that this Arabic-derived Persian script came much later after Islam. [22]

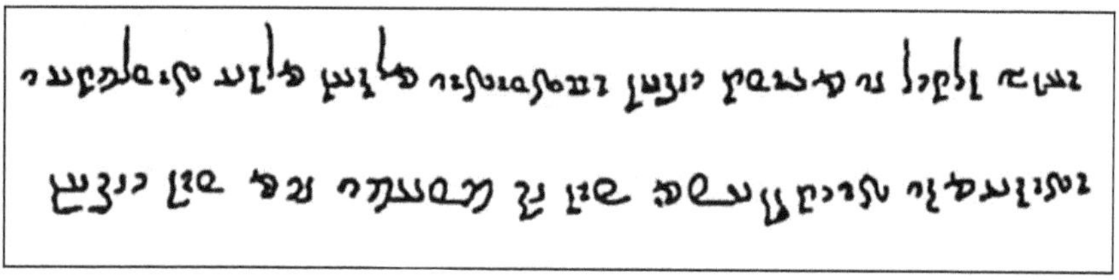

Figure (5.6) Kartirz Avesta inscription found on the Kabah of Zartusht. Dated to the 3rd Century CE. [5]

Figure (5.7) Taq e-Bostan Pehlavi inscription of Shapur III. Dated to late 3rd Century CE. [36]

Still, some theories on the origin of Arabic can support a possible early Persian influence, especially when considering that it is widely believed that the Arabic script, Jazm, was first used in *al-Ḥīrah* and *al-Anbār* areas of *Bilād al-'Irāq* (Iraq) which was under the Persian rule during that period. Others talk about *al-Kindī* script style in *al-Ḥīrah* as if it were existing, side by side the *Jazm* script style of *Ḥijāz* and *Bilād al-Shām* (Greater Syria.) [1] Some of the theories explored by *Ibn al-Nadīm,* had even listed pre-Islamic Arabic names and tribes from that same area who supposedly designed the early forms.

It is commonly believed today, that *Bishr bin 'Abd al-Malik al-Kindī,* maybe a Christian Arab, was the first to bring Jazm from *al-Ḥīrah* to Mecca. [15] *Bishr* was the brother of *al-Ukaydir,* a leader from ancient *Dawmat al-Jandal* (outside *Sakākah* of northern Saudi Arabia) that is located 200 miles southwest of *al-Ḥīrah. Dawmat al-Jandal* is the earliest known northern Arab city dating back to the 10th century BCE. [36] During the 5th - 6th century CE, *Dawmat al-Jandal* was the capital of the Arab kingdom of *Kindah.* The following is a famous pre-Islamic Arabic poem, attributed to a man from Mecca or *Dawmat al-Jandal,* which is widely referenced in Arabic literature today: [18]

لا تجحدوا نعماء بشر عليكمُ فقد كان ميمون النقيبة أزهرا

أتاكم بخط الجزم حتى حفظتموا من المال ما قد كان شتى مبعثرا

فأجريتم الأقلام عوداً وبدأة وضاهيتمو كتاب كسرى وقيصرا

وأغنيتمو عن مسند الحي حمير وما زبرت من الصحف أقيال حميرا

Below is a rough English translation of the above poem verses:

Do not deny *Bishr*'s* favors to you
He was a man of open blessed wisdom

* Bishr bin ʿAbd al-Malik

He brought you *Khaṭṭ al-Jazm* * that helped you save
The money that was plenty and scattered

*Arabic Jazm script style

You then moved the pens back and forth
As skillful as scribers of *Kisrâ** and *Qayṣar**

* Sassanid and Roman Emperors

And had no need to Musnad of father *Ḥimyr**
And whatever the Himyrite kings wrote on pages

* *Ḥimyr* tribes of Yemen

To facilitate the discussions in the next sections, I provided in Figure 5.8 a summery table containing a wide range of historical shapes of Jazm and Musnad Arabic letters, including cursive, side-by-side the most commonly referenced shapes of the Nabataean letters. These shapes were traced from various available Islamic and pre-Islamic inscriptions, manuscripts, and papyri, found throughout the greater Arabian Peninsula.

Please notice the many shapes of Musnad, including, but not limited to, those of Yemen.

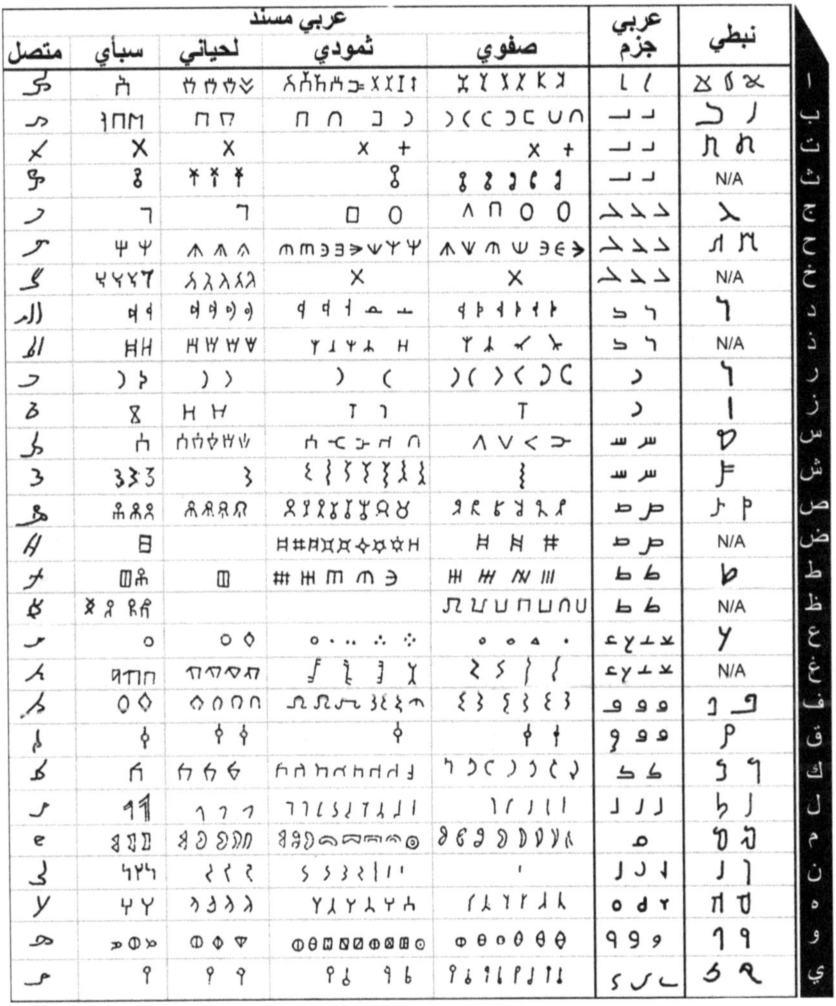
عربي مسند
متصل
سبأي
لحياني
ثمودي
صفوي
عربي جزم
نبطي
ا ب ت ث ج ح خ د ذ ر ز س ش ص ض ط ظ ع غ ف ق ك ل م ن ه و ي

Figure (5.8) Letter shapes of various Arabic Musnad styles and early Arabic Jazm traced from available modern evidence of inscriptions, manuscripts, and papyri shown side-by-side Nabataean and modern Arabic letters.

5.4 Roots of Jazm Script: Nabataean or Musnad?

Most scholars believe, that the modern Arabic script had evolved or transformed during the 4th century CE from either the Nabataean or Syriac script. On this issue, I beg to differ. A thorough examination of early relevant inscriptions and documents points to other roots. I am reasonably convinced that the early Arabic script, Jazm, was independently developed by the Arab tribes settling north of *Ḥijāz* and *Najd* from local versions of cursive flavors of Musnad, particularly the *Ṣafawī* style, much earlier than the 4th century CE. This is especially true when knowing that early Jazm shares with Musnad its representation of an exact 28 letters, albeit through a much lower number of shapes (around 14 shapes.) It also shares with it its early use of multiple shapes per letter that became widely used later on. It even used several Musnad shapes without major modifications. Jazm may have coexisted with and influenced by the more prominent Aramaic scripts that existed in its physical proximity — particularly the Nabataean. However, Jazm's approach to connectivity and shapes was quite different.

The way cursive Jazm flows along a horizontal line is unique. It lays letters' shapes on an exaggerated horizontal line employing smoother curves and even alternative shapes. It has a connectivity style and rhythm that can be better identified with that of cursive Musnad of Yemen, than cursive Nabataean, and it shares with it the use of extended horizontal strokes. Pointedly, while the Nabataean script connects vertical letters as they are, cursive Musnad significantly transforms them before joining. With a stretch of imagination, some Nabataean shapes can be made to resemble those of Jazm, but so do many Musnad shapes. Still, as stated earlier, shape's similarity is not the only indication of a script origin, especially since Nabataean, Aramaic, and Musnad, share the same roots.

In Arabic, the word Musnad means "supported", but in the context of a script, it means monumental (vertically standing like monuments.) Like Phoenician and Aramaic, Musnad was written with isolated letter shapes, and despite its occasional multi-ordering, it evolved to a primarily right-to-left script. Centuries later, like Phoenician and Aramaic, Musnad had witnessed the introduction of several derived yet distinct styles. Most notable were the northern *Liḥyānī* and *Ṣafawī*, and nomadic *Thamūdī*. It is a common mistake today to treat Musnad as a single style, *Saba'ī*, that is limited by single geographic area — south Arabia. By all accounts, Musnad was as prominent and alive in the northern Arabian Peninsula, as it was in the south.

Musnad inscriptions dated back to the 3rd century CE show advanced cursive forms, clearly illustrating its flexibility and adaptation. This highly cursive script, also known as South Arabian Minuscule or Popular Musnad, was used in old Yemen to inscribe daily documents on softer wood sticks. Standard Musnad was primarily used for rock-cut monumental inscriptions. [27] Clearly, Musnad was not sitting idle while its Aramaic relatives in the north being evolved into a variety of other forms (Nabataean, Syriac ...etc.) as many scholars imply today. Certainly, we cannot rule out, with any certainty, the development of a northern Musnad cursive style in the form of Jazm.

To the Arabs of *Ḥijāz* and the rest of the greater Arabian Peninsula, Yemen was always the heartland of Arabia. In 615 CE, when Prophet Muhammad wanted to protect his followers from prosecution in Mecca, he ordered them south towards Yemen and *Ḥabashah*, modern Ethiopia. Just as Yemen was (and still is) the Arab genealogical reference, its script was their reference script. As mentioned earlier, wherever they settled, the Arabs carried with them not only their language and gods, but also their scripts. While exposure to the old script among the tribes might have probably diminished — the further they moved north and away from their original population centers —, writing had most likely regained the central stage after the development of newer population centers extending as far north as the upper Euphrates River.

Like the word Musnad, the word Jazm most definitely had a direct script-related meaning. In fact, several pre-Islamic poems (like the one shown above) had mentioned both scripts explicitly. In classic Arabic, the root word *jazza* means "cut" to reduce size or volume of an existing object. For example, "*jazza al-karūf*" means "shear the sheep wool." The derived noun *Jazm* means "shortening" or "slashing." The new derived script was named "*Khaṭṭ al-Jazm,*" literally meaning "the slashing script," which is the Arabic way of saying the shortened script. Clearly, the inventors of Jazm must have referred to a newer script that have shortened another, probably by simplification and reduction of letter shapes. This can fit exactly what Jazm could have done in relation to Musnad, a much longer alphabet, but not to any short alphabet like Nabataean.

Figure (5.9) An old Yemen cursive Musnad Arabic inscription etched on wooden stick, dated early 3rd century CE. [27]

Jazm carries clear markings of an original and independent script. In all probability, the northern Arab inventors of *Jazm* were familiar with and even used Nabataean, the prominent script of the area; but at the same time, they surely seem to be as familiar with Musnad. Inscriptions show that they had actually used it during the Nabataean period. Even though some northern Arab population centers have clearly adapted Aramaic letters, the majority of the northern Arabs have also continued using Musnad. Musnad was widely inscribed on Arabian gods, from Yemen to Palmyra. The evidence is unambiguous: Musnad writings were on both early Jazm and late Nabataean inscriptions. In fact, Musnad was used until the early years of Islam.

Evidently, the development of Jazm was a continuous process spanning over several centuries. Early inscriptions before and after the advent of Islam included both isolated and attached forms of the same letters. It seems that Jazm had only matured after the emergence of the Early Kufic style. Although this style is named after *al-Kūfah* (Iraq), inscriptions dated to around 4 *Hijrī* calendar (625 CE) show that it was first used in *al-Madīnah al-Munawwarah* (Medina.) Like other religious groups who lived around them, the Muslims have apparently wanted to designate a distinctive style for the writing of their new book, the Quran. That the Arabic writing system reached its maturity only after the beginning of the Islamic era is a quite ordinary fact. Most scripts develop fully only after being adapted in a political state environment. Before Islamic, Jazm Arabic was clearly a developing script.

Summarizing my view on Arabic's Nabataean link, early inscriptions leave little doubt that Jazm was invented and/or developed in northern Arabia within the vicinity of Nabataean-dominated areas. Early Jazm inscriptions clearly indicated a trend for borrowing or mixing Nabataean letters on a temporary, as well as permanent basis. This practice seems common among other scripts in that area. The early Jazm shapes for the final letters *dāl*, *'ayn*, *wāw*, *tā'*, and *nūn* clearly resemble the Nabataean forms; but as indicated earlier these shapes can also be identified with Musnad.

Historically, the area controlled by the Nabataeans was known to be a sanctuary for those prosecuted by the Romans. Based on geography and accounts reported in the Roman history, it is beyond doubt that the overwhelming majority of the Nabataeans were ethnically Arab tribes who had adapted, earlier, much of the languages and scripts of the neighboring Aramaic population centers. Their adaptation to new cultures had not only set precedents to other Arab tribes in the north, but also created the open and much needed environment for the development of the new Jazm.

It is not hard to figure out when the Nabataean script ceased to exist. For a starter, assigning the earliest Jazm Arabic inscription the exact date of the latest Arabic Nabataean inscription (namely the year 328 CE of *al-Namārah*) is overtly fixed and farfetched. It leaves the misleading impression that the Nabataean script had transformed into Jazm Arabic. My argument is straightforward: since none of the other Aramaic scripts in the same geographic area transformed significantly to become a completely different looking script before the Islamic era, why would the Nabataean script then undergo any such transformation?

It is known that the Nabataean kingdom lasted from around 300 BCE until its annexation by the Roman Empire in the year 106 CE. The city of Petra, however, continued its role as an important population center in the area until the 6th century CE. [34] The question that we need to ask here is most concerned with logic: Why does it make any sense that well-established people abandon their own script abruptly just a few decades before Islam in favor of a significantly different one? One plausible answer to this question is a hypothesis: the gradual decline of the Nabataean civilization opened the doors for greater influence from surrounding Arab tribes, bringing in a newer and fresher script.

This could explain the reason why only a few Nabataean inscriptions were written in a relatively classic Arabic language. It may even explain why the late Nabataean inscriptions had significantly more cursive forms than the older ones. Among the Arab tribes of the former Nabataean areas, a newly arriving Jazm may have simply replaced the Nabataean script. Understandably, this argument does not exclude the possibility that Arabic was derived independently from the Nabataean script and co-existed with it before replacing it. However, this is very unlikely since the Nabataean civilization was in a decline state, which is hardly a favorable environment to develop a newer and significantly more defined script.

To shore up the above argument that the Nabataean script had actually adapted itself to the new Arabic, after the fall of Petra and the establishment of newer Arab kingdoms in the area, it is important to bring up what historians of the Islamic Arab civilization wrote shortly after the advent of Islam. According to their accounts, when the celebrated Muslim military leader *Khālid Ibn al-Walīd* advanced north toward Damascus, he encountered Arab tribes who did not speak in classic Arabic tongue. He asked them "Are you Arabs or Nabataeans?" They replied, "We are Arabs who were Nabatized, and Nabataeans who were Arabized." In reading the Arabic language of *Raqqūsh,* one can clearly hear the non-classic Arabic tongue once heard by *Khālid bin al-Walīd.* [18] It stands to reason to presume that the pre-Islamic "re-Arabization" of the Nabataeans had involved both their language and script.

Scholars of the early centuries of the Islamic Arab civilization era seemed to be well-informed about the origins and nature of the Nabataean people. Early accounts suggested that they were not purely Arabs, but mixed Arabs, like most of the Arab population in northern *Ḥijāz*, which was also referred to as *Nazār*. The *al-Fihrast* of *Ibn al-Nadīm* confirmed that the Nabataeans did not speak the Arabic of his time. It referred to *Ibn al-Waḥshiyah al-Kildānī,* from a city near *al-Kūfah*, as the translator of numerous Nabataean texts to Arabic. This translator was sometimes named *al-Kisdānī*, which seems to be a scribing error of the *kāf-lām* ligature. Quoting one of their magicians, *Ibn al-Nadīm* describes a typical Nabataean look as "black, barefoot, with cloven heels." As we saw in Chapter 2, *Ibn al-Nadīm* believes the Nabataeans were older than the Assyrians and Chaldeans. This would reinforce my earlier observation in section 5.2 that the Nabataean script seems to be much older than the Syriac script, contrary to today's common belief, which was put forward by the 19th century European theories.

When isolated, many Nabataean letters are almost identical to those of Aramaic or Aramaic Hebrew. Connectivity in late the Nabataean script seems as an afterthought. Clearly, as many inscriptions show, the Nabataeans were exposed to scripts that practiced connectivity, later. One such script could have been a cursive Musnad variant in the form of Jazm. A possible explanation could be that some Arab tribes, settling north, wanted to set their scripts apart from the surrounding Aramaic scripts by altering their script, Musnad, or by inventing a new one. It is useful to note that the cursive rules of the late Nabataean script show few similarities to those of early Arabic.

As stated above, numerous inscriptions from the Arabian Peninsula confirm that the northern Arab tribes had continued using Musnad. The Nabataeans could have embraced an Aramaic-like script to facilitate better communication and trade relations with the surrounding cities. Nevertheless, it seems that all along, they used two scripts. In truth, we cannot rule out that several Nabataean letters could have been derived directly from Musnad, too.

According to history sources, in the early centuries CE, Palmyra (*Tadmur*), a small kingdom north of the Nabataean area with a predominantly Arab population, used two writing systems: a monumental isolated script — Musnad —, and a cursive Mesopotamian script. This was probably due to its location on the trade route between Persia and the Roman Empire. It seems that they kept Musnad for formal religious use since most Palmyra gods had Musnad inscriptions. Even though the letters of their day-to-day script were clearly derived from the Aramaic script, the letters *thā'* and *rā'* were directly borrowed from Musnad. [30] [32]

It is important to observe that the available evidence confirming usage of Nabataean shapes in early Jazm inscriptions was limited, geographically, to areas of Nabataean influence. Also, it was limited to only a few pre-Islamic inscriptions. Therefore, one should not conclude with absolute certainty whether these shapes were representing the original Jazm shapes or just temporary locale ones, especially after examining early Islamic Jazm shapes, as will be seen later.

Before reviewing and discussing evidence presented by modern day discoveries of manuscripts, papyrus, and inscriptions, it is imperative to highlight the work, evidence, and theories presented by early prominent scholars of the Islamic Arab civilization regarding Musnad and the origins of Jazm. Although Musnad was discontinued after Islam, these scholars knew much about it, prior to the Western discoveries of the nineteenth century. Naturally (and without a doubt,) early scholars must had access to more and fresher information than we have today. While they had differed on the precise origins of Jazm as a writing style, most had taken for granted that it was of a Musnad background.

One such scholar was *Ibn al-Nadīm*. Evidently, he had direct access to major libraries of his time, including access to the manuscripts in the library of Caliph *al-Ma'mūn* palace. *Ibn al-Nadīm*'s father was a successful book collector. In his introduction to *al-Fihrast*, a multi-volume encyclopedic index of thousands of books and authors of his time, he explored different theories dealing with the origin of the Arabic script. While these theories differed on details, all seemed to indicate that the script was invented by Arab tribes in *Ḥijāz*, *Najd*, or other northern centers like *al-Ḥīrah* and *al-Anbār*.

Before giving his personal account, *Ibn al-Nadīm* wrote, "*Ḥimyar* used to write with the Musnad script with varied forms of *alīf*, *tā'*, *tā'*." (*Ḥimyar* refers to the people of pre-Islamic Yemen.) After explaining that he was put in charge of translating a Musnad manuscript from the *al-Ma'mūn* palace library, he sketched individual Musnad letters as he saw them; meaning, they were an exact reproduction of what was in the manuscript. Immediately after presenting the Musnad shapes, he gave his personal opinion. He wrote, "The first of the Arab scripts was the script of *Makkah*, the next of al-Madīnah, then of *al-Baṣrah*, then of *al-Kūfah*. For the *Alifs* of the scripts of *Makkah* and *al-Madīnah,* there is a turning of the hand to the right and lengthening of strokes, one form having a slight slant". He then provided an example. [22]

Another well-known Muslim scholar, *al-Hamadhānī*, had also provided sketches of the Musnad alphabet in his book, *al-Iklīl*, which he wrote in 950 CE. [18] His work confirmed *Ibn al-Nadīm*'s observation of the use of various shapes for the same letter in Musnad. In addition to *alif*, *bā'*, and tā', he listed various shapes for the letters *rā'*, *dhā'*, *zā'*, *lām*, *mīm*, *nūn*, and *hā'*. One interesting observation from his sketch was the use of three position-dependent shapes for the letter *hā'* in Musnad. Modern inscriptions had confirmed most of these shapes of Musnad as observed by both scholars. And, the smart note by *Ibn al-Nadīm* regarding right-slanted *alif* was

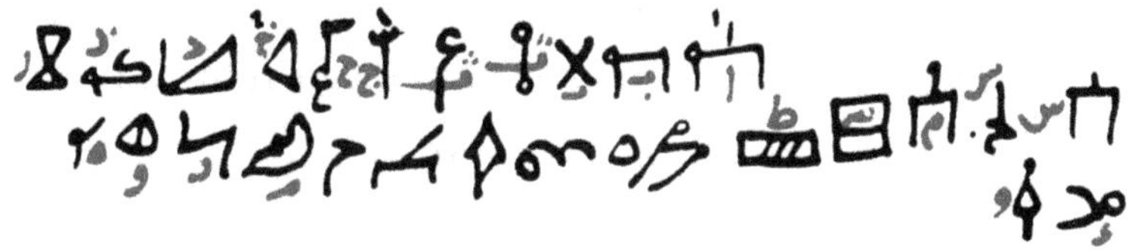

Figure (5.10) Arabic Musnad alphabet as sketched by *Ibn al-Nadīm* (d 990 CE) in his book *al-Fihrast* written around 970 CE. Letters order is that of old *Ḥijāz* and Tihāmah which is almost identical to the one used today by Arabic dictionaries. Arabic letters tinted by author. [22]

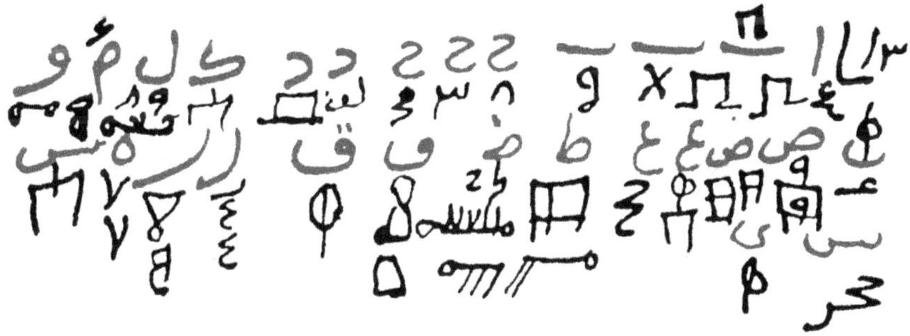

Figure (5.11) Arabic Musnad alphabet as sketched by *al-Hamadhāmī* in his book *al-Iklīl* written around 945 CE. [18] The Arabic letters are ordered here according to old Najd Arabic alphabet. [26] Arabic letters tinted by author.

also confirmed by all pre-Islamic Arabic inscriptions dating back to the fourth, fifth and Sixth centuries CE. The various shapes of Musnad letter *alif*, sketched by *al-Hamdhānī,* even included two such right-slanted *alifs*.

Additionally, the fact that the earliest Kufic inscriptions were in Medina, not *Kūfah*, indicates a trend of northward script movement from *Ḥijāz*, which was *Ibn al-Nadīm's* key observation. This fact should not exclude the possibility that Arabs elsewhere in the Peninsula could have invented Jazm but it was mastered in Mecca and developed into the mature *Ḥijāzī* style of Jazm before the arrival of Islam.

Several other prominent Muslim scholars believed Jazm Arabic was derived from Musnad. Among them were *Ibn Khaldūn* and *al-Qalqashandī*. They both wrote that Jazm was originally known in Yemen as *al-Khaṭṭ al-Ḥimīrī* and was brought later to *al-Ḥīrah* and *al-Anbār* areas of Iraq, before it was introduced to Mecca. [18]

5.5 Inscriptions, Manuscripts, and Papyrus Overview

There are eight pre-Islamic Jazm inscriptions available to researchers today. According to Western scholars, the oldest one is the *Jabal al-Ramm* inscription found east of Aqabah, Jordan. Even though it does not carry a date, it was assigned the year 328 CE (the date of *al-Namārah* Nabataean inscription, overly referenced as the proof of the Nabataean origin of Jazm!) The other possible earliest inscriptions are the two found in *al-Sakākah* of northern Saudi Arabia; dated back to the 4th or may be early 5th century CE. Another possible earliest inscription may also be the Arabic *Umm al-Jimāl* inscription found south of Damascus and dated around the fifth century (this is not the same as the *Umm al-Jimāl* Nabataean inscription, which we studied in Chapter 3.) Then we have the recently discovered *al-Jazzāz* inscription dated 410 CE. The remaining three inscriptions are all dated back to the 6th century CE. The first one was a trilingual inscription (Greek, Syriac and Arabic) found in *Zabad* of northern Syria — dated back to 512 CE. The second was found near *Jabal al-Usays,* south of Damascus — dated back to 528 CE. The third was found in *Ḥarrān*, also south of Damascus — dated back to 568 CE. Only the inscriptions of *Usays* and *Ḥarrān* explicitly mentioned dates. The date of the Arabic text in the multilingual *Zabad* inscription was secured by the Greek text.

It must be noted that dating inscriptions is *dependent* on how scholars read their contents. The implication is immediate: precise dates can be unavoidably inaccurate, and even subjective. Each of the stated dates in *Usays* and *Ḥarrān* had two isolated segments following the word "*Sanat*" (Arabic for year.) Experts read the two parts combined as the Nabataean numbers, 423 and 463, which, of course, should be open to investigation. Looking from right to left, the assumption was that the first part in both inscriptions referred to the number 400, despite clear visual differences between the two. The first part in *Ḥarrān* could be a Nabataean number 200, or even the Arabic word *naḥw* for "approximately", "about", or "toward." It is not excludable that the last identical portion of the second parts could have been a reference to a year or event, rather than the Nabataean number 23.

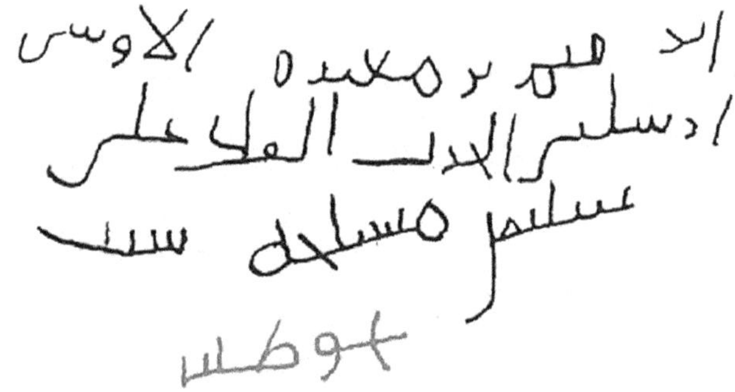

Figure (5.12) Pre-Islamic Arabic Jazm inscription of *Jabal al-Usays* found south of Damascus, Syria. Dated 528 CE. [28] Year is tinted by the author.

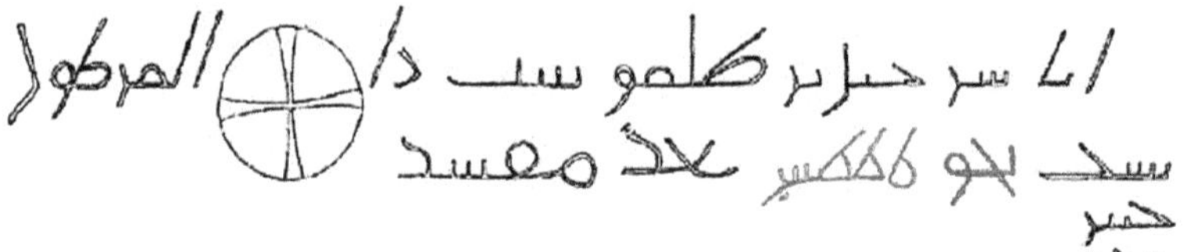

Figure (5.13) Pre-Islamic Arabic Jazm from a Greek-Arabic bilingual inscription found in *Ḥarrān*, south of Damascus, Syria. Dated 568 CE. [28] Year is tinted by the author.

Another note of relevance: no pre-Islamic Arabic inscriptions were found in the area around *al-Ḥīrah* and *al-Anbār*, in Iraq. The closest ones found are those of *al-Sakākah*, approximately

200 miles southwest of *al-Ḥīrah*. The absence of these inscriptions may indicate that no more inscriptions could be found there, and that Jazm came later. Still, this conclusion is doubtful — many important scholars believe that Jazm was used first among the Arab tribes in that area.

As for the Nabataean, numerous inscriptions (dating as early as the 3rd century BCE) are available today; but only four — out of several thousands found — had classic-like Arabic text, according to Western scholars. [13][35] These are frequently presented as evidence that Jazm was derived or evolved from Nabataean. The oldest one had only two Arabic text lines and it was found in *Ein Avadat*, currently Israel (dated to 88 – 150 CE) The second is the Nabataean *Umm al-Jimāl,* found south of Damascus (dated around 250 CE.)

Then there is the *Raqqūsh* inscription found in *Madā'in Ṣāliḥ* in northern Ḥijāz, Saudi Arabia (dated to 267 CE.) This onc has a summary in *Thamūdī* Musnad script. It also contains rarely-seen-before dots for a few letters. Some see *Raqqūsh* as a proof for the transformation of Nabataean to Jazm. It is said to represent the earliest Arabic forms. [13][35] Incidentally, it is not very peculiar to see dots in the *Raqqūsh* inscription. As stated earlier, dots are a pre-Islamic invention. Persian scripts like Pahlavi and Avesta may have used dots earlier. The script of Palmyra included dots, which may have been picked from Persian controlled Mesopotamia. [31] It is very likely that dots were passed to the late Nabataean via Palmyra.

The fourth is the famous *al-Namārah* Nabataean inscription. Some suppose that this inscription represented a "developed form of Nabataean alphabet, well on its way to becoming Arabic." [6] As we discussed in Chapter 3, many believe this was the stone placed on the tomb of *Umru'ū al-Qays*, the well-known pre-Islamic Arab king of *al-Ḥīrah* (not the same as *Umru'ū al-Qays,* the famous pre-Islamic Arab poet from *Kindah,* who lived in the sixteen century CE.)

Undisputedly, all the pre-Islamic inscriptions listed above are very important tools in the study of early Arabic development. Depending only on these few inscriptions, however, is insufficient and even misleading. First, etching letters on hard surfaces can significantly distort the intended forms. Second, by referencing just a few inscriptions, we may not have enough data to make informed conclusions, since only few shapes are revealed. Third, all referenced inscriptions belonged to a limited geographic area — this limitation would make a comprehensive study impossible to achieve.

To be effective, a balanced study of Arabic script's origins must examine letterforms of the early Islamic decade's documents, as well, simply because they are abundant and show shapes that are more precise than those on stone medias. It is not clear as to why no pre-Islamic inscriptions on such medias are available, especially knowing that we do have Arabic papyri from as early as the second decade of the Islamic *Hijrī* calendar. (You may recall that *Ibn al-Nadīm* wrote about his handling of a pre-Islamic Musnad manuscript.)

The two earliest post-Islamic Arabic inscriptions were found in *al-Madīnah* and are dated back to the fourth year of the *Hijrī* calendar (625 CE.) Both have reasonably developed early Kufic shapes. [11] There is also the *Zuhayr* inscription dated 25 *Hijrī* (642 CE,) which was discovered in Northern *Ḥijāz*. This inscription mentioned the name of the second Muslim Caliph, *'Umar Ibn al-Khaṭṭāb* and the year he died. Then there is *al-Ḥijrī* grave inscription of Egypt, dated to 31 *Hijrī* (652 CE,) followed by *Darb Zubaydah* inscription found in *Wādī al-Shāmiyyah*, *Ḥijāz*, and dated 40 Hijri (660 CE.) Also from *Ḥijāz*, we have the *Wadī Sabīl* inscription, which belongs to 46 *Hijrī* (666 CE.) From Palestine, we have the *Ḥalḥūl* inscription dated 55 *Hijrī* (674 CE) and an undated inscription found in the *Nūba* village (near Hebron,) which also mentions the name of the second Muslim Caliph, *'Umar Ibn al-Khaṭṭāb*. This could make it the second or third oldest Islamic inscription. Among the early Islamic inscriptions, we also have the *Mu'āwiyah* Dam inscription from *Ṭa'if*, *Ḥijāz*, dated 58 *Hijrī* (677 CE) and the *Karbalā'* inscription of Iraq, near *al-Kūfah*, dated 64 *Hijrī* (683 CE.) Then we have the famous Dome of the Rock inscription in Jerusalem, which we will discuss further later, dated 72 *Hijrī* (692 CE.) Finally, we have two more undated inscriptions, which believed to be from the early Islamic decades.

As for non-inscription medias from the early decades of the Islamic *Hijrī* calendar, we have at least five letters by Prophet Muhammad, allegedly in the handwriting of his cousin *'Alī bin Abī Ṭālib.* To facilitate an in-depth discussion, I shall provide detailed images and transcriptions of two of these letters in section 5.6. The two letters contain valuable shapes (like *hā'* and *'ayn*) and can shed light on the shape characteristics of the day-to-day Arabic script in *Ḥijāz.* One letter was sent to *al-Mundhir ibn Sāwī,* ruler of Bahrain and conqueror of *al-Ḥasā',* and the second to the Byzantines emperor, *Hirqal* (Heraclius). It is believed that Prophet Muhammad sent a total of 15 letters to neighboring leaders. [15]

A plethora of other post-Islamic evidence dating back to the first few decades of Islam is also available to researchers. Among these are the two earliest Arabic papyri dated to 22 *Hijrī* (642 CE.) One is a bilingual inscription including Greek writing, which can be found today in the Austrian National Museum, Vienna. The two were account settlement documents related to purchase agreements or taxes. Not surprisingly, the two papyri listed above included clear dots on several letters confirming the fact that dots were used commonly before the fifth decade of the Islamic era when they were officially institutionalized or at least acknowledged.

Several early papyri of the Quran (most written in the early Kufic style) are also available. One Quran papyrus from Medina was identified by some as an example of a rare, short-lived, *Mā'il* (slanted) calligraphic style and was dated back to the 8th century. [25] My belief though, after studying its letter shapes and because of its deliberate slanted style, it is much older — probably mid 7th century CE. The defining characteri-

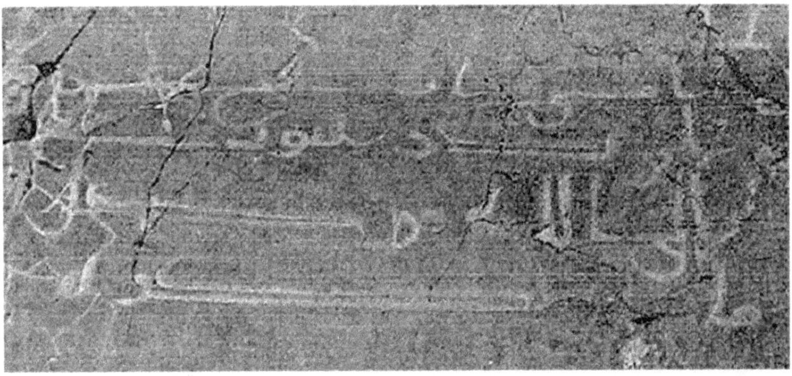

Figure (5.14) One of the two earliest Arabic Kufi inscriptions found in Mount *Sal'*, Medina. Dated 4 Islamic *Hijrī* calendar (625 CE.) [28]

Figure (5.15) Early Arabic Kūfī inscription on a rock in *Ṭa'if*, Saudi Arabia. Dated to the early decades of Islam. [20]

Figure (5.16) Undated Arabic inscription found in *Nūba* village (near Hebron), Palestine, which mentions the name of the second Muslim Caliph, *'Umar bin al-Khaṭṭāb*.

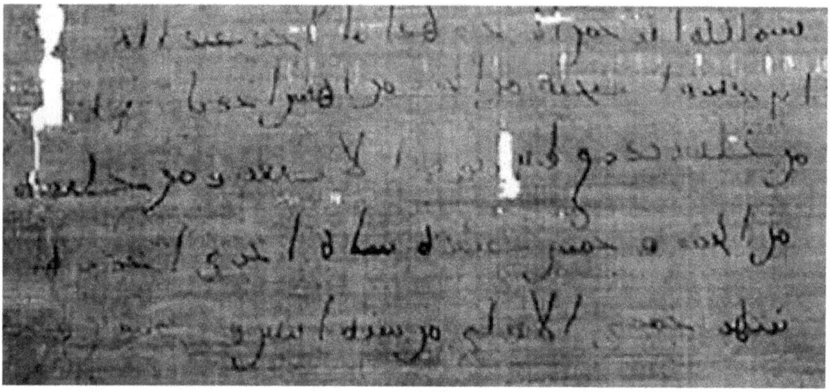

Figure (5.17) From the earliest Arabic papyrus dated 22 *Hijrī* calendar (642 CE,) containing Arabic and Greek text. Kept in the Austrian National Museum, Vienna. [28]

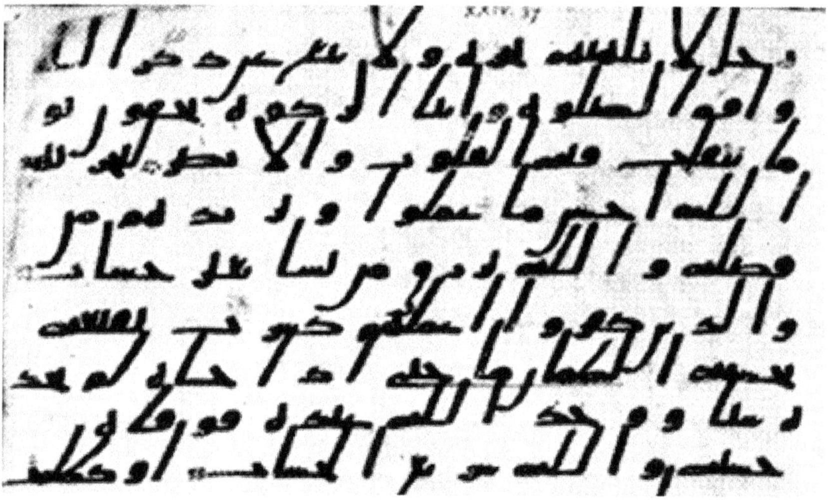

Figure (5.18) From an early Quran (24.37) papyrus page written in Medina, Saudi Arabia, in the *Mā'il* calligraphy style that included "hidden" dots. Dated back to the 8th century CE, but the author believes it is older. [25]

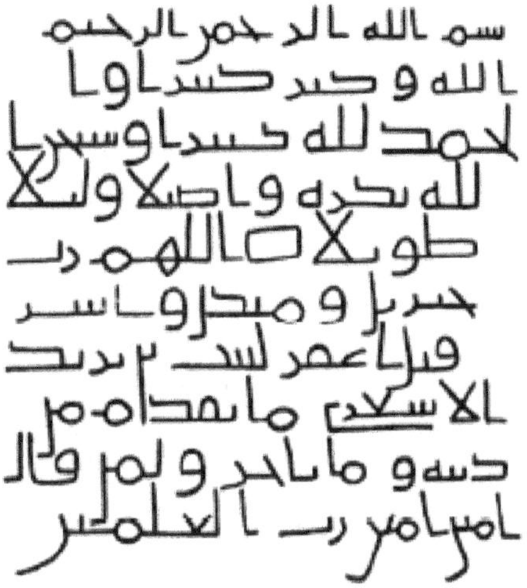

Figure (5.19) Arabic Kufic inscription found near Karbalā´, Iraq, dated 60 *Hijrī* (683 CE.) Notice the use of letter *wāw* in *Allāh akbar* on the second line. [28]

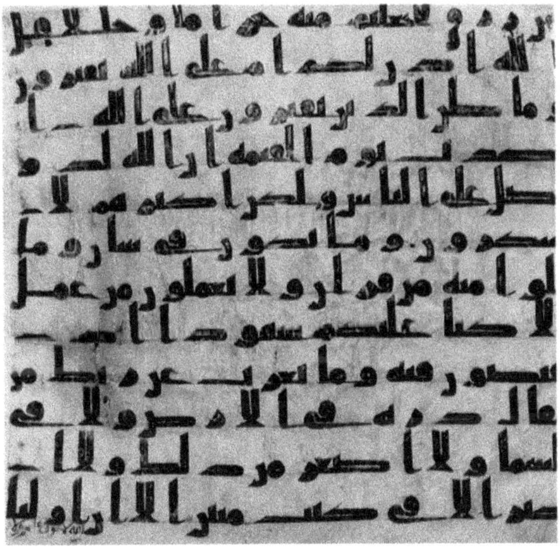

Figure (5.20) From a page of one of the earliest Quran (10.59) on parchment, written with early un-dotted Kufic style in Medina, Saudi Arabia. Dated to mid-7th century CE. [14]

stics of the letterforms of this Quranic papyrus are almost identical to that of the two earliest papyri mentioned above, and that of the early Kufic style seen in one the oldest copies of the Quran, which is recorded on parchment and kept today in the Egyptian National Library, Cairo. [14]

The important inscription found on the outer and inner mosaic of the octagonal arcades of the Dome of the Rock in Jerusalem is well preserved and rather long. Its letterforms are clearly those of the *Māʾil* style but without the slant. This inscription included early diacritic usages. The text of the inscription is *du'ā'* دعاء, which is a form of Islamic prayer that typically includes a mixture of Quranic and non-Quranic passages. The subject of the Quranic passages of the text revolved around the Islamic interpretation of Jesus, which clearly was targeting the sizable Christian community of Jerusalem. The use of *du'ā'* in inscriptions and the recital of their text during religious occasions was (still is) common in the Muslim world. To inform the reader, the earlier Kufic inscription near *Karbalā'*, Iraq, also included *du'ā'*.

Curiously, the inscription at the Dome of the Rock was a main ingredient of the latest Western "academic coup d'état" (led by a group of German researchers) in the field of Arabic and Islamic studies, as we discussed in Chapter 2. Taking advantage of Western readers' unfamiliarity with the concept of Islamic *du'ā'*, some put forward an unsubstantiated claim that the Quran did not exist in the period when this inscription was made, that is, during the rule of Umayyad Caliphate. Despite abundantly available information and material evidence indicating otherwise, these scholars continue to claim that the passages in this inscription were "proto-ingredients" incorporated into what was to become the Quran *after* the advent of the Abbasid Caliphate in 750 C.E.

Figure (5.21) Part of the inscriptions at the Dom of the Rock in Jerusalem dated to 64 *Hijrī* (684 CE). Top from the west and northwest mosaic of the inner octagonal arcade (notice the third word *'āmanū*.) Bottom from the west and northwest outer octagonal arcade. [28]

The striking facts about the early post-Islamic evidence regarding the Arabic script include the rich and culturally diverse use of shapes, limited or slightly differing shapes per letter, and loose observation of connectivity. To substantiate this, earlier Musnad or Nabataean shapes in various positional forms are very easy to spot. Clearly, even in the early decades of Islam, the Arabs were interchanging letter shapes using a large cache of forms they were exposed to previously. A few examples include the use of final *yā'*, medial *'ayn*, medial *hā'*, ligature of medial *bā'* before *rā'*, and the medial *qāf* of Kufic style. One could argue whether these shapes had come from Nabataean or Musnad; the fact remains, ascribing immunity to Jazm from the influence by either script is a false assumption.

5.6 Examining the Musnad Roots of Jazm

Despite clear evidence of a Nabataean script influence, after studying both Islamic and pre-Islamic inscriptions, papyri, and manuscripts, one concludes that Jazm was, undeniably, a Musnad Arabic script derivation. Identical letter shapes, like *rā'*, *wāw*, *'ayn*, and *hā'*, were used in Jazm even after Islam. By examining Musnad shapes and its variants including cursive styles, we can easily uncover common visual characteristics with Jazm and later calligraphic styles like Kufic. All of the following letters in Jazm, shīn, *yā'*, *mīm*, *lām*, *'ayn*, *hā'*, *jīm*, *fā'*, *qāf*, *dhāl*, *zā'*, *kāf*, and *nūn*, can be traced back to Musnad.

The extent of the transformation that Musnad shapes underwent throughout the centuries supports the hypothesis of a Musnad transformation to Jazm. Evidence shows that a typical scriptural transformation process can involve flipping and rotating shapes, along with minor or major elimination of components. For example, in both Greek and Latin, early Europeans flipped and otherwise transformed the adapted Phoenician (or possibly Musnad) letters to form their early scripts. Many centuries later, they repeated the same process with the Arabic numerals. When examining the shapes of the current Arabic numerals 2 and 3, for instance, it is evident that the two numerals resemble the exact shapes of the Arabic-Indic numbers 2 and 3, rotated 60-90 degrees counterclockwise! With Musnad, such a transformation process could have been achieved by rotating vertical letters to assume horizontal positions, and by eliminating those parts that interfere with a smooth cursive writing process and/or with recognition and differentiation of letters' shapes.

The earliest Arabic inscription of *Jabal al-Ramm* does not include clear letterforms to study. Yet, it is important since it includes a mixture of Arabic Musnad and Jazm letters. H. Grimme believed the Arabic Jazm text was inscribed earlier. Bellamy, on the other hand, thought otherwise. Strangely enough, while both diametrically differed in how to read the Arabic text, they both agreed to ignore discussing the Musnad text. *Mādūn* believes this inscription is the missing link between Jazm and Musnad — in essence, he read both texts as one. My take on the issue is practical: I believe that letters of both scripts were inscribed at the same time, and that the value of this inscription is due, primarily, to the presence of Musnad and primitive Jazm shapes, together. As mentioned earlier, the *Raqqūsh* Nabataean inscription included Musnad and Nabataean appearing side by side. Since no one questioned its presence in the *Raqqūsh* inscription, why should we then question it in *Ramm*, especially when knowing that the quality of shapes of both texts is identical, and that the usage of random text direction within one inscription is quite common in old Arabia?

Figure (5.22) The earliest pre-Islamic Arabic Jazm inscription found near *Jabal al-Ramm*, east of *'Aqabah*, dated 328 CE. From a photograph by Lankester Harding.

One of the two *Sakākah* inscriptions used a Musnad shape for the Arabic medial letter *hā'*. Khalil al-Muaikel spelled the top word of that iscription as *ba'*, *'ayn*, *sīn*, and *wāw*, assumingly referring to a name, *ba'sū* بعسو However, this non existing name does not sound Arabic at all. Besides, the third letter does not even remotely resemble any Arabic or Nabataean shape for the letter *sīn*. Reading a slightly raised area as middle tooth of an Arabic letter *sīn*, in an inscription full with similar slightly raised areas, is to say it nicely, bizarre. Clearly, this letter looks more like a Musnad letter *ha'*. The word is probably bāʻahū باعهُ or *biʻhū* بِعهُ meaning "sold him" or "sell him", respectively. Reading this word in this manner would, at least, match the current reading of the inscription that deals, supposedly, with a slave of *Umru'ū al-Qays*. Incidentally, the sole comparison of how the name *Umru'ū al-Qays* was written in the Nabataean *al-Namārah* and the Arabic *Sakākah* inscriptions, only a few decades apart, leaves us with the impression that Nabataean could not have transformed to Jazm, but instead, it co-existed and interacted with it.

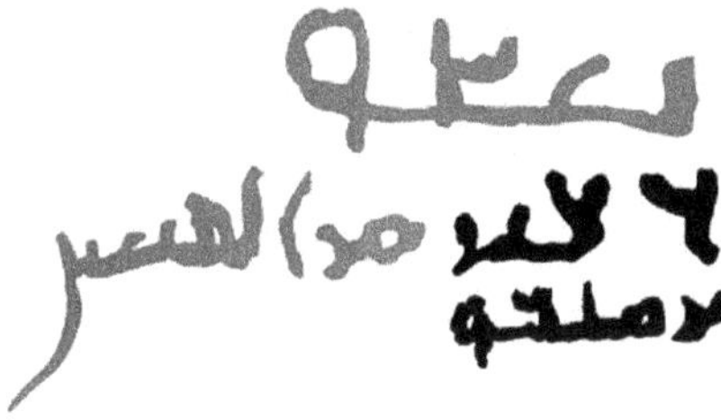

Figure (5.23) One of two pre-Islamic Jazm inscriptions found in *Sakākah*, Saudi Arabia. Dated 4th or early 5th century CE. [28] The words *bi'hū* (or *bā'ahū*) with medial Musnad letter *hā'* (top) and *Umru'ū al-Qays* (middle) are tinted by the author.

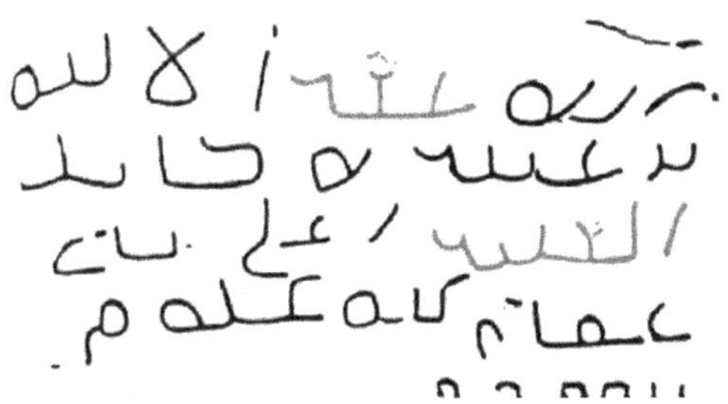

Figure (5.24) Pre-Islamic Jazm inscription of *Umm al-Jimāl* found south of Damascus, Syria. Dated 4th or 5th century CE. The words *'ahada* and *al-hunayd*, with medial Musnad letter *hā'* are tinted by the author. [18]

Among all pre-Islamic Jazm inscriptions, the *Umm al-Jimāl* Arabic inscription is probably the most significant and controversial. Although many scholars differed on its date, the majority believe that it belongs to the 5th or 6th century CE. Some refer to it as the *Umm al-Jimāl al-Thānī* (*Umm al-Jimāl* the Second) to distinguish it from the earlier Nabataean *Umm al-Jimāl* inscription. It seems that this inscription used multiple shapes for *hā'* in its final, medial, and isolated forms — twice each. This usage clearly confirms *al-Hamadhānī* and *Ibn al-Nadīm*'s sketches of multiple Musnad *hā'* shapes. In addition, these medial shapes clearly match those seen in several letters by Prophet Muhammad, written a century later (see Figures 5.25 - 5.29.)

Two of these letters (Figures 5.25 and 5.26) were traced and examined thoroughly by the author. The two included eight words with initial and medial Musnad letter *hā'* shapes. Words with initial and medial Musnad letter *hā'* are circled by the author for clarity. The bottom re-tracings in both images were compared to multiple original copies. The tracing of Figure 5.25 was compared to an original copy kept in the private collection of *Hinrī Fir'awn*, a Lebanese citizen. [18] Words with medial Musnad letter *hā'* are: al-*hudá* الهدى and *ishhadū* اشهدو. The tracing of Figure 5.26 was compared to the shown original photograph. [16] Words with initial and medial Musnad letter *hā'* are from right to left and top to bottom: *ishhad* اشهد, *amruhum* امرهم, *lahum* لهم, *ahl* اهل, *minhum* منهم, and *mahma* مهما.

Today, many read the second word of the first line of the Arabic *Umm al-Jimāl* inscription as *ghafara* غفر and the first word of the third line as *al-khulayd* الخُليد or *al-qulayd*

القُليد. From my perspective, and based on the overwhelming evidence regarding the Musnad letter *hā'*, I read the first word as *'ahada* عَهَدَ or *'ahuda* عَهُدَ, and the second *al-hunayd* الهُنيد. Reading a Nabataean *rā'* in *ghafara* would contradict the current reading of all previous and subsequent inscriptions. Jazm had consistently used Musnad *rā'*, as is, in all available inscriptions, let alone early Islamic inscriptions. Besides, in Arabic, the word *ghafara* means "forgave." *Mādūn* argued that *ghafara* in that context meant "to protect" or "to keep safe". This interpretation, however, does not reflect, not even minimally, the standard transmitted meaning of the word. In fact, the words *'ahada* and *satara* are more commonly used to convey the meaning that Mādūn suggested it implies.

Incidentally, well-known Western Arabist, Bernard Lewis, and most other Western scholars claim that Prophet Muhammad's surviving letters are forged and devoid of any historical value. In contrast, Muslim historians generally affirmed their existence and authenticity. Of course, this dismissive Western scholarly attitude toward past Islamic Arab scholarship is very typical, as we discussed in earlier chapters. Nevertheless, the unique handwriting and shapes seen in these letters clearly attest their genuineness. It is difficult to imagine why would one forge these letters by writing the Arabic letter *ha'* in its Musnad shape, *in all of them*, many centuries *before* the modern debate about the origin of the Arabic script had started. The mere fact that all these letters have contained an identical seal with the words *Muḥammad Rasūl Allāh* unusual-

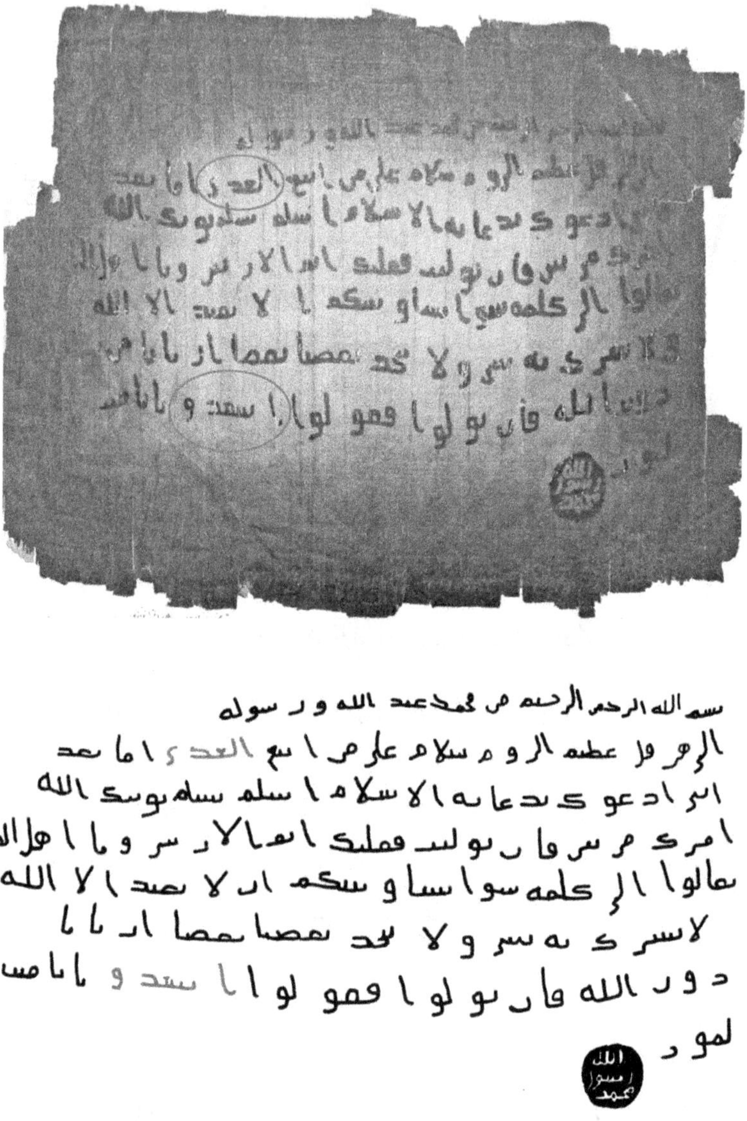

Figure (5.25) Original copy of Prophet Muhammad letter to the Byzantines Emperor, Heraclius, owned by a Yemeni family (top.) [29] Letter was delivered by *Diḥyah ibn Khalīfah al-Kalbī* to his minister at *Tabūk*. Words with letter *hā'* are circled and tinted by the author. [15]

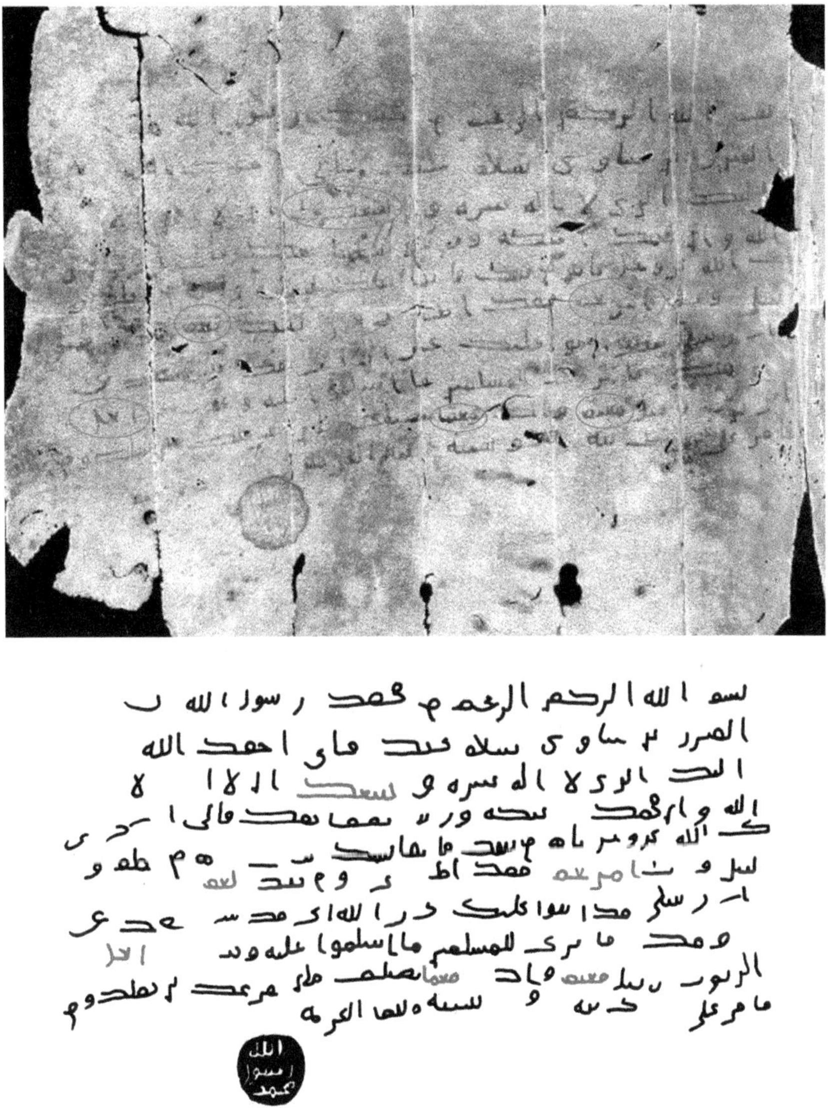

Figure (5.26) Photograph of Prophet Muhammad's letter to *al-Mundhir ibn Sāwī*, ruler of Bahrain (top,) kept in the Iraqi Museum, Baghdad, or Tob Qabi Museum, Istanbul, according to other sources. Letter was delivered by *'Alā' ibn Ḥadhramī*. Words with letter *hā'* are circled and tinted by the author. [15]

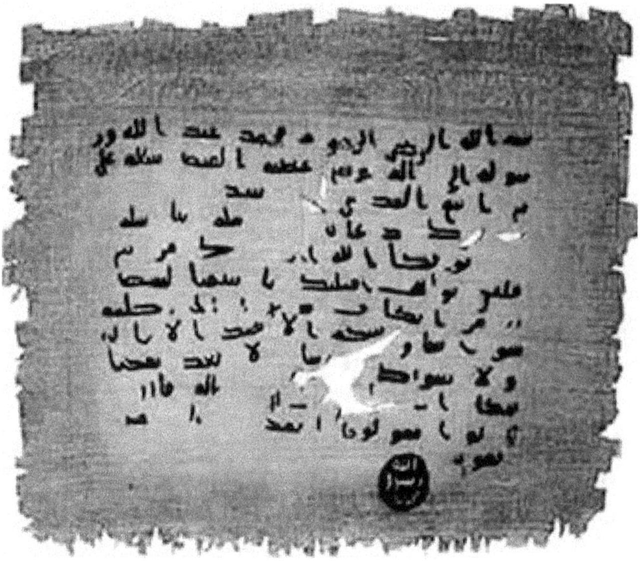

Figure (5.27) Photograph of Prophet Muhammad's letter to *al-Muqawqis*, Quptic ruler of Egypt, kept in Tob Qabi Museum, Istanbul (top.) An original traced copy of the letter (bottom). [36]

Figure (5.28) Prophet Muhammad's letter to *al-Hārith bin Shimr al-Ghassānī*, King of *al-Ḥīrah*, Iraq. [36]

Figure (5.29) Prophet Muhammad's letter to *Musaylamah al-Kadhdhāb* [36]

ly ordered vertically from bottom to top, a known Musnad Arabic practice, is quite significant. Aside from confirming their authenticity, it indicates that early Arabic Jazm script was heavily shaped by Musnad.

Additionally, evidence that early Arabic was independently derived from a cursive Musnad background can be seen in its usage of a unique slanted *Alif* shape, resembling one of the variant *Alif* shapes used by the northern *Ṣafawī* Musnad style. That *Alif* was slanted to the right with an angle identical to that of a slanted cursive Musnad, in all available pre-Islamic Arabic inscriptions. Even *al-Hamadhānī* noticed that in his sketch of Musnad shapes. My point: it is extremely unlikely that the small Nabataean shape of looped *Alīf* (commonly placed much higher above the base line) could have transformed into Jazm *Alif*.

Finally, the most compelling evidence connecting Jazm to cursive Musnad can be seen in how it joins letters along an exaggerated, straight horizontal line. The same extended, open-ended, horizontal strokes seen to the left of almost every cursive Musnad letter are also seen is early cursive Jazm letters. This distinguished approach of Jazm sets it apart from Nabataean or other scripts in the area. Although it is reasonable to hypothesize that sometime during the 3rd century, the Nabataeans began altering their letters' shapes to achieve full horizontality, the same, however, can be argued for Musnad.

5.7 Conclusion

The modern Arabic script was originally called *Jazm* to differentiate it from the historical, pre-Islamic Arabic script called *Musnad*. Western scholars of the 19th century claimed that Jazm had evolved from the late Nabataean script. Their theories were formalized after Dussaud's discovery of *al-Namārah* Nabataean inscription and were further emphasized after the discovery of *Raqqūsh* and *Umm al-Jimāl* which we studied in detail in Chapters 3 and 4. To their credit, not all contemporary Western scholars, who linked Arabic to the Nabataean script, claim that Nabataean transformed into Arabic. Such claim would discard, completely and unfairly, the centuries old testimonial accounts developed by prominent scholars of the Islamic Arab civilization era, asserting that Arabic was derived from *Musnad*. Other Western scholars advance just one theory positing that the Arabic script was derived from the Nabataean script. Such theory could be sustained because it does not contradict with the possibility of Jazm being co-derived from other scripts used in the region.

In my view, the Arabic Jazm script was *independently* derived around the 3rd century CE, possibly in *al-Ḥīrah* area of Iraq (*Tannūkh* Kingdom era,) from the Arabic Musnad script, with strong Nabataean and even Sassanid and Syriac scripts influence. The evidence that Jazm was an independent script is attested by the fact that it had initially consisted of only 14 undotted shapes, not the usual 22 shapes of the Aramaic scripts, to reduce or slash the number of letters of the Musnad script,

28 letters. The word Jazm, which means "slashing" in the Arabic language, is clearly referring to a matrix script with a much larger number of letter shapes, like Musnad.

Linking early Arabic solely to the Nabataean and Syriac Aramaic scripts because of a few cursive inscriptions, is not sufficient to prove it was one of their adaptations since during that time the use of cursive styles was gaining ground very rapidly in the whole Near East. In fact, one cannot rule out the possibility that the Aramaic script itself was derived directly from Musnad, or indirectly through Phoenician, as we explained in section 5.2. In Yemen, according to available inscriptions, cursive *Musnad* became popular around the 3rd century CE. About the same time, Sassanid Avista inscriptions were heavily cursive. Even earlier, the *Tadmur* Kingdom (Palmyra) used a cursive Mesopotamian script.

Between the 2nd and 4th century CE, the latest north-migrating Arab tribes did not rely initially on writing as a means of expression, like most Arab tribes did outside their original population centers. However, when they needed to write, they used *Musnad*. Evidence of this can be found in the thousands of Musnad inscriptions discovered in northern Arabia. This can explain the scarcity of non-Musnad Arabic Jazm inscriptions. Additionally, depending on where they lived, the northern Arabs have also used the scripts of adjacent areas, like the Nabataean script in the ex-Nabataean lands, and Aramaic in central and northern Iraq (*Haḍar,*) and eastern Syria (*Tadmur.*)

Jazm, it seems, was originally invented by someone familiar with Musnad, Nabataean, and other popular scripts of the area. It was probably used first in a limited manner in *al-Anbār* and *al-Ḥīrah*, and slowly moved to the old Nabataean areas and the rest of the Arabian Peninsula in the mid 3rd century CE, the time of *al-Namārah,* and similar inscriptions.

The Nabataean script lost its prominence after the 2nd century CE, following the fall of Petra kingdom in 105 BCE, but continued its reluctant journey to becoming cursive around the 3rd century CE (the evidence of *Raqqūsh* and *Umm al-Jimāl* inscriptions.) It is possible that in the late 2nd century CE, when the Nabataeans came under the influence of the *Tannūkh* Arab kingdom based in *al-Ḥīrah,* they have gradually replaced their script in favor of the newly emerging Jazm. They have possibly adapted the cursive rules of the newly invented script, initially, as it is clear in *al-Namārah*, before abandoning their script all together. The *Jazm* Arabic used in the ex-Nabataean areas was clearly influenced by the reluctantly-cursive shapes of the late Nabataean script, which were eventually incorporated in the future Arabic Naskh calligraphy style that was fully developed, according to most Arabic calligraphy historians, during the Islamic Umayyad era in Damascus, Syria.

Originally, the Jazm script had most likely resembled the early Kufic style, which clearly had the imprints of Musnad, not early the Naskh style. Jazm was brought to Mecca in the late 5th century CE from the *Ḥīrah* area, not Syria. The young script was not fully developed until after Islam, in *Ḥijāz,* where it was used to write the original copies of the Quran. This is apparent since the *Ḥijāzī* Jazm style was called *Kūfī* to indicate that its origin was the city of *al-Ḥīrah* — which was replaced after Islam by the newly built city of *al-Kūfah*, located only few miles north.

In its early existence, Arabic Jazm could have been just a local northern cursive Musnad style. Arguably, Musnad was not standing idle while its relatives, Phoenician and Aramaic scripts, were all evolving into a variety of styles. Because of their nomadic nature, the northern Arab tribes were exposed to a wide range of neighboring letterforms that had affected Jazm development. Evidently, the lack of utilization by a powerful central state had prolonged the Jazm development cycle.

It is not clear which northern Arab tribes had first used Jazm. This is not important, though, since despite their vast geographic area, these tribes enjoyed very close ties. Most definitely, the emergence of pre-Islamic Mecca as a prominent trade and worship center had played a major role in the forming and spreading of Jazm, to the extent that it became known as the script of *Ḥijāz.* The Arab tribes of *al-Ḥīrah* could have been the originators of Jazm, or the ones who had significantly transformed it. However, the direct predecessor of modern Arabic was the Jazm style of *Ḥijāz.* As stated earlier, the Arabic script have only developed into a solidly defined script after the emergence of Islam, when a derived style, early Kufic, became the official and religious script of the new Islamic Arab state.

Early Jazm Arabic script was a script of powerful shapes and dynamics. Being a true regional product shaped by the forms of both Musnad and Aramaic Nabataean, it quickly established itself as the unifying script of the greater Arabian Peninsula, North Africa, and Persia. In as little as two centuries after the advent of Islam, Arabic became a worldwide prominent script with rich, calligraphic traditions. The older scripts of the area that survived through present time were significantly affected by its success. Most importantly, with the expansion of Islam, even distant nations adapted the Arabic script shapes. This is expected since, for many centuries, and in vast regions around the world, Arabic became the undisputed script for science and culture.

Bibliography

1. Abuhaiba, Ibrahim S. I. "A Discrete Arabic Script for Better Automatic Document Understanding." *The Arabian Journal of Science and Engineering* 28 (2003): 1B.
2. Ancient Hebrew Research Center. Museum of Hebrew Script. "Alphabet." http://www.ancient-hebrew.org
3. Ancient Scripts. "Pahlavi." http://www.ancientscripts.com/pahlavi.html
4. "Arab Calligraphy: Portrait of Magnificence, Majesty, and Grace." *Areen: Arabcin's Monthly Magazine* 25 (2001.) http://www.arabcin.net/areen/areen_english/25/cover1.htm
5. Avesta. "Zoroastrian Archives." http://www.avesta.org

6. Bellamy, James A. "The new Reading of al-Namarah Inscription." *Journal of the American Oriental Society.* 105 (1985): 31-48.
7. Bellamy, James A. "Two Pre-Islamic Arabic Inscriptions Revisited." *Journal of the American Oriental Society.* 108, no.3 (1988): 369-378.
8. The Catholic Encyclopedia. "Petra." http://www.newadvent.org/cathen/11777b.htm
9. Farrokh, Rokn od Din Homayun. *History of Book and the Imperial Libraries of Iran.* Tehran: Ministry of Art and Culture, 1963.
10. Forvm Ancient Coins. "Nabataean Numerals and Number Words." http://www.forumancientcoins.com
11. Hamidullah M. "Some Arabic inscriptions of Madinah of the early years of Hijrah." *Islamic Culture.* XIII (1939): 427-439.
12. Healey, John F., and Han J. W. Drijvers. *The Old Syriac Inscriptions of Edessa and Osrhoene.* Brill, 1999.
13. Healey, John F. *The Nabataean Tomb Inscriptions of Mada'in Salih.* Journal of Semitic Studies, Supplement 1. London: Oxford University Press, 1993.
14. Hussein, Mohamed A. *Origins of the Book: From Papyrus to Codex.* Greenwich, Connecticut: New York graphics Society Ltd., 1970.
15. Islamic Civilization. http://www.cyberistan.org/islamic/letters.html
16. Khan, Gabriel Mandel. *Arabic Script: Styles, Variants, and, Calligraphic Adaptations.* New York: Abbeville Press Publishers, 2001.

17. Khan, Majeed. *The Origin and Evolution of Ancient Arabian Scripts.* Riyadh: Ministry of Education and Department of Antiquities and Museums, 1993.
18. Mādūn, Muḥammad ʻAlī. *Khatt al-Jazm ibn al-Khatt al-Musnad.* Dimashq: Dar Ṭlās lil-Dirāsāt wa al-Terjamah wa al-Nashr, 1989. First Edition.
19. McGuire, Gibson. "Nippur." The Oriental Institute of the University of Chicago. 2001-2002 Annual Report. http://oi.uchicago.edu/research/pubs/ar/01-02/nippur.html
20. Miles, G. C. "Early Islamic Inscriptions Near Ta'if in the Hijaz." *Journal of Near Eastern Studies.* VII (1948): 236-242.
21. al-Muaikel, Khalil. "Pre-Islamic Arabic Inscriptions from Sakaka, Saudi Arabia." *Studies on Arabia in honor of Professor G. Rex Smith. Journal of Semitic Studies Supplement* 14 (2002): 157-169. London: Oxford University Press, 2002.
22. al-Nadīm, Ibn. *The Fihrest of al-Nadim.* Translated and Edited by Bayard Dodge. New York: Columbia University Press, 1970.
23. OmniGlot: Writing Systems and Languages of the World. "Avestan." http://www.omniglot.com
24. Rostovtzeff, M. I. "The Caravan Gods of Palmyra." *The Journal of Roman Studies. Part 1: Papers Dedicated to Sir George MacDonald* 22 (1932): 107-116.
25. Safadi, Y. H. *Islamic Calligraphy.* Boulder: Shambhala Publications Inc, 1997.
26. al-Saggār, Muḥammad Saʻīd. *Abjadiyyat al-Saggar: al-Mashruʻ wa-al-Miḥnah.* Dimashq: Dar al-Mada, 1998.

27. Al-Said, Said F., and Stefan Weninger. "Eine Unvollendete Sabäische Urkunde." *Arabian Archaeology and Epigraphy* 15 (2004) 68-71.
28. Saifulla, M. S. M., Muhammad Ghuniem, and Shibli Zaman. "From Alphonse Mengana to Christoph Luxenberg: Arabic script and the alleged Syriac Origins of the Quran." Islamic Awareness website. http://www.islamic-awareness.org
29. al-Sālim, Wārid Badir. "Makhṭuṭah Takshif 'Anhā al-Zamān." *al-Zamān Arabic Daily Newspaper.* 10, no. 2725 (June 19, 2006.) UK Edition.
30. Segal, J. B. "Four Syriac Inscriptions." *Bulletin of the school of Oriental and African Study, Fiftieth Anniversary* 30 no. 2 (1967): 293-304. University of London.
31. Segal, J. B. "Some Syriac Inscriptions from the 2nd - 3rd Century A. D." *Bulletin of the school of Oriental and African Study* 16 no. 1 (1954): 13-36. University of London.
32. Sheridan, Susan Guise, Ph.D. University of Notre Dame. Department of Anthropology. "Pictures from a trip to Petra." http://www.nd.edu/%7Esheridan/Jordan%202000/Jordan%202000.html
33. Smithsonian. National Museum of Natural History. Written in Stone: Inscriptions from the National Museum of Saudi Arabia. http://www.mnh.si.edu/epigraphy/
34. Starcky, Jean. "The Nabataean: A Historical Sketch." *The Biblical Archaeologist* 18 no. 4 (December 1955.)
35. al-Theeb, S.A. "Two New Dated Nabataean Inscriptions from al-Jawf." *Journal of Semitic Studies* XXX|X (1994): 33-40.
36. Wikipidia. The Online Encyclopedia. http://en.wikipedia.org

ABOUT THE AUTHOR

Arabic type designer, independent researcher, librarian, and systems engineer. Born 1958 in Sacramento, California, and grew up in Karbala and Baghdad, Iraq. Moved in 1979 to New York, where he earned a Bachelor of Science in Electrical Engineering and a Master of Science in Library and Information Sciences. Served for 12 years as a Senior and Supervising Librarian in the New York Public Library, specializing in Arabic, Science, and Business subjects. Served for 15 years as a Systems Librarian and a library Director of Technology in the City University of New York (CUNY.) A known and active Arabic type designer especially noted for his non-traditional, innovative, Arabic typeface designs. Awarded a US design patent in 2000 and a utility patent in 2003 for his Mutamathil Type Style, an open template for simplified, technology-friendly, Arabetic font designs. Released more than 30 original typeface families, since 1992. Published several articles in scholarly journals about Arabic script's history, typography, and computing. Contributes regularly to discussions of Arabic related topics on international typography and archeology forums.

www.ingramcontent.com/pod-product-compliance
Lightning Source LLC
Chambersburg PA
CBHW070911100426
42814CB00003B/128
* 9 7 8 0 9 8 4 9 8 4 3 0 5 *